Science

Imponderables®:
Science

Collins gem

David Feldman

IMPONDERABLES®: SCIENCE. Copyright © 2006 by David
Feldman. All rights reserved. Printed in the United
States of America. No part of this book may be used or
reproduced in any manner whatsoever without written
permission except in the case of brief quotations
embodied in critical articles and reviews.
For information, address HarperCollins Publishers,
10 East 53rd Street, New York, NY 10022.

HarperCollins books may be purchased for educational,
business, or sales promotional use. For information,
please write: Special Markets Department,
HarperCollins Publishers, 10 East 53rd Street,
New York, NY 10022.

FIRST EDITION

ISBN-10: 0-06-089886-0
ISBN-13: 978-0-06089886-1

06 07 08 09 10 ❖/WOR 10 9 8 7 6 5 4 3 2 1

A confession. I spent my entire academic life avoiding science classes. And when I couldn't avoid required courses, I suffered through them, memorizing lists of species and chemical symbols that I didn't understand. I thought I wasn't interested in science.

Then I got into the business of answering mysteries for a living. I've devoted the last twenty years of my life to writing books that attempt to eradicate the little mysteries of everyday life that drive us nuts. And more than a few of these questions fell into the realm of science. Even if I wasn't interested in studying Bernouli's Principle or Einstein's Theory of Relativity, I want to know why we look up when thinking, or why the moon seems to follow you when you're driving on the highway.

I repent. To answer a question about how our world works, you need science. It's amazing how interesting a subject can be when you actually want to know how to solve a problem. Several of the scien-

tists who I've contacted for the ten *Imponderables*®
books confided that they pursued the study of
science because they were obsessed with their own
Imponderables, little mysteries that had no practical
application.

The good folks at Collins suggested collecting my
favorite science Imponderables together for this Gem
edition. With a few exceptions, the text is unchanged
from the original editions.

Almost all the questions in this book came from
readers. Besides the release of psychic stress, the
first to pose each mystery received a free, autographed copy of the book. Do you have any
Imponderables hounding you, about science or any
other subject? You can be rewarded, too. Come join
us on the Web at www.imponderables.com, e-mail us
at feldman@imponderables.com, or if you must
resort to the Imponderable institution known as the
United States Postal System, write to us at:

Imponderables
P.O. Box 116
Planetarium Station
New York, NY 10024-0116

The expression *partly sunny* was brought to you by the same folks who brought you *comfort station* and *sanitary engineer*. As a technical meteorological term, *partly sunny* doesn't exist. So while you might assume that a partly sunny sky should be clearer than a partly cloudy one, the two terms signify the same condition. You have merely encountered a weathercaster who prefers to see the glass as half full rather than half empty.

Actually, most of the meteorological terms that seem vague and arbitrary have precise meanings. The degree of cloudiness is measured by the National Weather Service and described according to the following scales:

Percentage of Cloud Cover	Term
0–30	clear
31–70	partly cloudy
71–99	cloudy
100	overcast

Where does "fair" weather fit into this spectrum? Fair weather generally refers to any day with less than a 50 percent cloud cover (thus even some "partly cloudy" days could also be "fair"). But even a cloudy day can be termed fair if the cover consists largely of transparent clouds. On days when a profusion of thin cirrus clouds hangs high in the sky but does not block the sun, it is more descriptive to call it a fair day than a partly cloudy one, since one thick cloud formation can screen more sunshine than many willowy cirrus formations.

You might also have heard the aviation descriptions of cloud cover used in weather forecasts. Here's what they mean:

Percentage of Cloud Cover	Term
0–9	clear
10–50	scattered clouds
51–89	broken sky
90–99	cloudy
100	overcast

Not many people know what the weather service means when it forecasts that there is a "chance" of rain. Precipitation probabilities expressed in vague adjectives also have precise meaning:

Chance of Precipitation	National Weather Service Term
0–20%	no mention of precipitation is made
21–50%	"chance" of precipitation
51–79%	precipitation "likely"
80–100%	will not hedge with adjective: "snow," "rain," etc.

How does the National Weather Service determine the daily cloud cover in the space age? Do they send up weather balloons? Satellites? Not quite. They send a meteorologist to the roof of a building in a relatively isolated area (airports are usually used in big cities) and have him or her look up at the sky and make a well-informed but very human guess.

The movement of the straw depends upon the liquid in the glass and the composition of the straw itself. The rapidly rising straw phenomenon is usually seen in glasses containing carbonated soft drinks. Reader Richard Williams, a meteorologist at the National Weather Service, explains the phenomenon:

> ...the rise occurs as carbon dioxide bubbles form on both the outside and inside of the straw. This increases the buoyancy of the straw and it gradually rises out of the liquid.
>
> The gas is under considerable pressure when the drink is first drawn or poured. When that pressure is released the gas forms small bubbles on the sides of the glass and on the straw. As the bubbles grow the straw becomes buoyant enough to "float" higher and higher in the container.

Occasionally, though, a straw will rise in a noncarbonated beverage, and we didn't get a good explanation for this phenomenon until we heard from Roger W. Cappello, president of strawmaker Clear Shield National. We often get asked how our sources react to being confronted with strange questions. The only answer we can give is—it varies. Sure, we like authoritative sources who fawn over us and smother us in data. But we must confess we have a special place in our hearts for folks like Cappello, who make us sweat a little before divulging their secrets. Here is his letter to *Imponderables*, verbatim, skipping only the obvious pleasantries:

> After pondering your question for a while, I decided to toss your letter as I was too busy for this. I later retrieved the letter and decided I would attempt to give you an answer that is slightly technical, mixed with some common sense and some B.S.
>
> First off, I know the action you were referring to had something to do with "specific gravity." Specific gravity, as defined by Webster, is "the rate of the density of a substance to the density of a substance (as pure water) taken as a standard when both densities are obtained by weighing in air."
>
> Straws today are formed from polypropy-

lene, whereas many years ago they were made of polystyrene, before that paper, and before that, wheat shafts.

Assuming water has a specific gravity of 1, polypropylene is .9, and polystyrene is 1.04. A polypropylene straw will float upward in a glass of water, whereas a polystyrene straw will sink. However, a polystyrene straw will float upward in a carbonated drink as the carbonation bubbles attach themselves to the side of the straw, which will help offset the slight specific gravity difference between water and polystyrene. A polypropylene straw will float higher in a carbonated drink for the same reason. If you put a polypropylene straw in gasoline, and please don't try this, it will sink because the specific gravity of gas is lighter than water.

If you lined up ten glasses of different liquids, all filled to the same level, the straws would most likely float at all different levels due to the different specific gravities of the liquids and the attachment of various numbers of bubbles to the straws.

I really wish you hadn't brought this up as I'm going to lunch now. I think I'll order hot coffee so I can ponder the Imponderables of my business without distraction.

Good luck.

We can use all that good luck you were wishing us. I'm sure you had a productive lunch, too. Anyone willing to share information with us can eat (and sleep) with a clear conscience, knowing that he has led to the enlightenment of his fellow humans.

Submitted by Merrill Perlman of New York, New York.

WHY CAN'T YOU SEE STARS IN THE BACKGROUND IN PHOTOS OR LIVE SHOTS OF ASTRONAUTS IN SPACE?

There actually are folks out there who believe that NASA pulled off a giant hoax with the "so-called Moon landings." Often, the lack of stars in the background of photos of the astronauts is cited as startling evidence to support the conspiracy.

Sheesh, guys. If you want to be skeptical about something, be dubious about whether "When you're here, you're family" at Olive Garden, or whether State Farm Insurance will be there for you the next time you're in trouble. But don't use a dark background in a photo of outer space to convince yourself that astronauts have never gotten farther into space than a Hollywood soundstage.

The answer to this Imponderable has more to do with photography than astronomy. Next time you go to a football game on a starry night, try taking a photo of the sky with your trusty 35mm point-and-shoot camera or camcorder. Guess what? The background will be dark—no stars will appear, let alone twinkle, in the background.

The stars don't show up because their light is so dim that they don't produce enough light on film in the short exposures used to take conventional pictures. But you have seen many photos of stars, haven't you? These were undoubtedly time-lapse photographs, taken with fast film and with the camera shutter left open for at least ten to fifteen seconds. Without special film and a long exposure time, the camera lens can't focus enough light on the film for the image to appear. Jim McDade, director of space technology for the University of Alabama at Birmingham, elaborates:

> Even if you attempt to take pictures of stars on the "dark side" of the Earth during an EVA [an extra-vehicular activity involving astronauts leaving the primary space module, such as a spacewalk] in low-earth orbit, a time exposure from a stable platform of about twenty seconds is necessary in order to capture enough stellar photons to obtain an image showing stars, even when using fast films designed for low-light photography.

The same problems occur with digital cameras, film, and video cameras, as McDade explains:

> A digital camera, a film camera, and the human eye all suffer similar adaptability problems when it comes to capturing dimmer background objects such as stars hanging behind a space-walking astronaut in the foreground. The human eye is still much more sensitive than the finest digital or film camera.
>
> Photographic film is incapable of capturing the "very bright" and the "very dim" in the same exposure. The lunar surface is brilliant in daylight. The photos taken by the Apollo astronauts used exposure times of a tiny fraction of one second. The stars in the sky are so dim that in order to capture them on film, it requires an exposure time hundreds of times longer than those made by the Apollo astronauts.

Those of us who live in the city have had the experience of going out to a rural area on a clear night, and being amazed at the number of stars we can see when there aren't lights all around us on the ground. You can create the same effect inside your house. On a clear night, kill the lights in a room and look out the window. Depending upon the atmospheric conditions, a star-filled sky may be visible to you. Flip on the lights inside the room, look outside, and the stars have disappeared.

Why? Light from a bright object near us can easily dwarf light emanating from distant objects, such as stars. In the case of astronauts, the lights attached to the space vehicle or space station or even the lights on an astronaut's helmet can wash out the relatively dim light from the stars in the background.

Even with sensitive film, the suits that astronauts and cosmonauts wear reflect a lot of light. The glare from the astronauts themselves will provide contrast from the dark sky background and faint stars. Any light emanating from the stars is unlikely to be exhibited when cameras are geared toward capturing clear shots of a space walker.

Perhaps the space conspiracists would stifle themselves if the Apollo astronauts had taken time-exposure photographs that could display the stars in all their glory, but they never did. As McBain puts it: "After all, they went to the Moon to explore the moon, not to stargaze."

Submitted by Scott Cooley of Frisco, Texas. (For much more information on the issues of photography in outer space, see Jim McDade's "Moonshot" Web site at http://www. business.uab.edu/cache/Defaultb.htm.)

WHY DO SONIC BOOMS OFTEN COME TWO AT A TIME?

Sonic booms are caused by the displacement of air around an aircraft flying faster than the speed of sound. Even slow-moving aircraft can produce pressure waves ahead of and behind the aircraft that travel at the speed of sound. But once supersonic speeds are attained, pressure disturbances called "shock waves" form behind the aircraft and reach the ground in the form of a thunderlike sound.

Many parts of the airplane are capable of creating shock waves, even the wings. But as the distance between the airplane and a person on the ground increases, only two shock waves are felt—the bow shock wave and the tail shock wave. Bill Spaniel, public information coordinator of Lockheed Aeronautical Systems Company, sent a clipping from *Above and Beyond: The Encyclopedia of Aviation and Space Sciences, Vol. II*, that explains the phenomenon:

> As the distance between the airplane and the observer is increased, the distance between the

bow and tail shock waves is also increased. A person on the ground may even hear two booms, with a time interval between the bow shock wave and the tail shock wave of one-tenth to four-tenths of a second.

These shock waves pattern themselves in a cone shape, and can be felt on the ground for miles on either side of the flight path.

If you haven't noticed an increase in sonic booms since the introduction of the Concorde, the explanation is that supersonic aircraft travel at heights often twice that of subsonic widebodies. Although just as many shock waves are created at 65,000 feet altitude as at 30,000 feet, the intensity of the sonic boom is diminished by the extra mileage down to the ground.

Submitted by Dr. J. S. Hubar of Pittsburgh, Pennsylvania.

Be the life of your next party. Buy a few rolls of
wintergreen Life Savers Roll Candy, cut all the
lights, gather your friends in front of you, and bite
down hard and fast. You'll sparkle in the dark. Your
mouth will glow bluish-green.

The explanation for this delightful phenomenon

comes directly from the research and development department of Life Savers Inc., which is now a division of Nabisco Brands:

> Our manager of Candy Technology tells us that two ingredients are necessary for this reaction. The sparkling comes about because of a combination of mint flavoring and crystalline sugar. When you crack the crystal, the energy then stimulates a component in the flavoring to emit a light. The component in wintergreen is methyl salicylate.

There are two possible hang-ups in producing the sparkling effect. First, the background atmosphere might not be dark enough (closets and bathrooms are highly recommended). Second, moisture seems to absorb the energy needed to produce sparkling. Do not expect good results in a sauna.

Our idea of a good time does not include trying to do long division with Roman numerals. Can you imagine dividing CXVII by IX and carrying down numbers that look more like a cryptogram than an arithmetic problem?

The Romans were saved that torture. The Romans relied on the Chinese abacus, with pebbles as counters, to perform their calculations. In fact, Barry Fells, of the Epigraphic Society, informs us that these mathematical operations were performed in Roman times by persons called "calculatores." They were so named because they used *calcule* (Latin for pebbles) to add, subtract, multiply, and divide.

Submitted by Greg Cox of San Rafael, California.

WHAT ACCOUNTS FOR THE GREAT DIFFERENCE IN CLIMATE BETWEEN THE ATLANTIC COAST AND PACIFIC COAST OF THE U.S.?

If you are like us, you glaze over during weather-casts on the local news. The intricacies of the weather map, complete with air flows and troughs, strike us as no easier to comprehend than quantum physics. Why waste five valuable minutes on a weather report when all we want to know is whether we need an umbrella or an overcoat? After all, the four minutes saved could be devoted to more important news, like a graphic depiction of another grisly murder or a juicy political scandal.

"It Never Rains in Southern California," warbled Albert Hammond in his 1972 gold record. Not quite accurate, Albert, but not a bad meteorological generalization from someone who spent most of his life in Gibraltar. The weather is more moderate on the left coast and certainly much warmer in winter. Why is this?

The one principle we have managed to glean from those weathercasts is that the prevailing winds in North America move from west to east. We inherit the weather from the west of us. The sea is much slower to change in climate and temperature than land masses. Although the Pacific Ocean has its share of storms, they are relatively infrequent and are usually associated with moderate weather. So the West Coast receives relatively infrequent storms and moderate weather.

Sol Hirsch, executive director of the National Weather Association, told *Imponderables* that the Rocky Mountains are most responsible for the colder and stormier weather of the East Coast (and the Midwest, for that matter):

> The weather in the east is determined by storm systems developing from the Rockies eastward that are generally moving in easterly or northerly directions, due to the rotation of the earth. In addition, the area east of the Rockies is exposed to cold air coming from Canada whereas cold air west of the Rockies is infrequent.

The collision of multiple fronts east of the Rockies

manufactures storms and makes the weather patterns volatile and difficult to predict.

Of course, the volatility of weather in the East makes the job of a weathercaster considerably dicier than his West Coast counterpart's. If a weathercaster in southern California predicts "85° and partly cloudy" during the summer and "75° and partly cloudy" during the other three seasons, he won't be too far wrong.

We could produce water by combining oxygen and hydrogen, but at quite a cost financially and, in some cases, environmentally.

Brian Bigley, senior chemist for Systech Environmental Corporation, says that most methods for creating water are impractical merely because "you would need massive amounts of hydrogen and oxygen to produce even a small quantity of water, and amassing each would be expensive." Add to this the cost, of course, of the labor and equipment necessary to run a "water plant."

Bigley suggests another possible alternative would be to obtain water as a by-product of burning methane in an oxygen atmosphere:

> Again, it's a terrible waste of energy. Methane is a wonderful fuel, and is better used as such, rather than using our supply to produce H_2O. It would be like giving dollar bills to people for a penny to be used as facial tissue.

The most likely long-term solution to droughts is desalinization. We already have the technology to turn ocean water into drinking water, but it is too expensive now to be commercially feasible. Only when we see water as a valuable and limited natural resource, like oil or gold, are we likely to press on with large-scale desalinization plants. In northern Africa, water for crops, animals, and drinking is not taken for granted.

Submitted by Bill Irvin III of Fremont, California.

The kiddie equivalent of the drunken partygoer putting a lampshade on his head is ingesting helium and speaking like a chipmunk with a caffeine problem.

Still, many *Imponderables* readers want to know the answer to this question, so we contacted several chemists and physicists. They replied with unanimity. Perhaps the most complete explanation came from George B. Kauffman:

> Sound is the sensation produced by stimulation of the organs of hearing by vibrations transmitted through the air or other mediums. Low-frequency sound is heard as low pitch and higher frequencies as correspondingly higher pitch. The frequency (pitch) of sound depends on the density of the medium through which the vibrations are transmitted; the less dense the medium, the greater the rate (frequency) of vibration, and hence, the higher the pitch of the sound.
>
> The densities of gases are directly propor-

tional to their molecular weights. Because the density of helium (mol. wt. 4) is much less than that of air, a mixture of about 78 percent nitrogen (mol. wt. 28) and about 20 percent oxygen (mol. wt. 32), the vocal cords vibrate much faster (at a higher frequency) in helium than in air, and therefore the voice is perceived as having a higher pitch.

The effect is more readily perceived with male voices, which have a lower pitch than female voices. The pitch of the voice [can] be lowered by inhaling a member of the noble (inert) gas family (to which helium belongs) that is heavier than air, such as xenon (mol. wt. 131.29)....

Brian Bigley, a senior chemist at Systech Environmental Corporation, told *Imponderables* that helium mixtures are used to treat asthma and other types of respiratory ailments. Patients with breathing problems can process a helium mixture more easily than normal air, and the muscles of the lungs don't have to work as hard as they do to inhale the same volume of oxygen.

Submitted by Jim Albert of Cary, North Carolina. Thanks also to James Wheaton of Plattsburg AFB, New York; Nancy Sampson of West Milford, New Jersey; Karen Riddick of Dresden, Tennessee; Loren A. Larson of Altamonte Springs, Florida; and Teresa Bankhead of Culpepper, Virginia.

The operative word in this mystery is *seem*. For all of our meteorological experts agree with Harold Brooks, the head of the Mesoscale Applications Group of the National Severe Storms Laboratory in Norman, Oklahoma, who states:

> There is a myth that tornadoes don't hit downtowns, but that is just a myth that comes from the fact that downtowns are small areas. If you randomly picked any other similarly sized areas in the middle of the United States, they wouldn't get hit often, either.

In other words, tornadoes are non discriminatory offenders, and are subject to the laws of probability. The land covered by major population centers is tiny compared to the total expanse of North America, but a big city is theoretically just as likely to get hit as all the local trailer parks if they covered as much of an expanse as the downtown area.

There are portions of the United States where tornadoes are much more likely to hit, however. Tornadoes have been tracked in all fifty U.S. states, but the so-called tornado alleys are the midwestern area from Texas all the way north to the Canadian border, in the southeastern United States, and in the Ohio Valley and southern Great Lakes region, extending as far east as western Pennsylvania. But within that general area, trailer parks, skyscrapers, the Mississippi River, or the Dallas Cowboy cheerleaders can't stop tornadoes.

One other reason why the perception may have spread that tornadoes don't hit big cities is that many of the densest population centers, such as the Washington, D.C.–to–Boston and the San Diego–to–San Francisco corridors, are outside of "tornado alley." Even so, tornadoes do sock big cities. Chuck Doswell, senior research scientist at the Cooperative Institute for Mesoscale Meteorological Studies, wrote us:

> Tornadoes have recently hit the downtown areas of such cities as Salt Lake City, Utah; Miami, Florida; Nashville, Tennessee; and Fort Worth, Texas. In the Texas event, there were at least two tall buildings hit. One suffered enough

damage that it was decided to demolish it rather than to repair the damage.

In 1970, in Lubbock, Texas, a violent tornado hit a large building with sufficient force to twist the structure. The only reason tall buildings are hit infrequently is that they don't occupy very much space in this nation of ours. The more area covered, the greater the likelihood of being hit by a tornado.

Dr. T. Theodore Fujita, a tornado scientist who developed the scale commonly used to rank the severity of tornadoes, considered the role of skyscrapers and population density in thwarting the development of small tornadoes. The University of Chicago professor, who died in 1998, noted that since 1921, "practically no tornadoes occurred or moved across the central portion of Chicago." Fujita theorized that perhaps the city's higher temperature than surrounding areas (a phenomenon we discussed in our *Imponderables* book *Why Don't Cats Like to Swim?*) and its man-made structures might be "acting against any tornado activity over the city." Other major population centers that have been studied for tornado patterns, London and Tokyo, also seem to enjoy a relative dearth of small-tornado activity. But no expert seems to seriously think that even the highest skyscraper in the largest metropolis would scuttle an intense tornado from unleashing its fury.

Submitted by John Beton of Chicago, Illinois.
Thanks also to Laura Gunn of Ames, Iowa.

Eleganza Shop

Featuring our "Food Fight" sheath

Bright color areas of SET-IN stains from blueberry, coffee, ketchup, more!

NO TWO DRESSES ALIKE $119.

First the good news. As you increase the temperature of the water applied to a stain, the solubility of the stain also increases. Obviously, dissolving the stain is a good first step in eliminating the stain.

Now the bad news. In practice, most of the time,

"dissolving" the stain translates into *spreading* the stain. Usually, hot water helps break up the stain, but it doesn't lift the stain; rather, it allows stains to penetrate deeper into the fiber. Oily stains, especially on synthetics, have this reaction. Once the stain sets deeply enough in a fabric, detergents or dry cleaning are often ineffective.

In other cases, hot water can actually create a chemical change in the stain itself that hampers removal. Protein stains are a good example of this problem, as Lever Brothers spokesperson Sheryl Zapcic illustrates:

> One common type of stain that can be set by hot water is a protein stain. If protein is a component of the stain, rinsing with hot water will coagulate the protein. For example, egg white, which is a protein, can be loosened with cold water without coagulating; however, hot water will immediately coagulate the egg white. Technically, this is called denaturation of the protein. In any event, the stain becomes insoluble or set.

On some stains, it won't matter much whether hot or cold water is used.

Our own rule of thumb on this subject is: Nothing works. We have been in fancy French restaurants where our dining companions insist that "only club soda can get that stain out of your tie." Of course, we never have club soda at hand. To placate our true believer, we end up ordering a glass. And, naturellement, the stain lingers as an enduring testament to our naïve belief that we will one day get a stain out of a garment successfully.

Submitted by Pamela Gibson of Kendall Park, New Jersey.

This Imponderable was posed by a caller on John Dayle's radio show in Cleveland, Ohio. John and the supposed Master of Imponderability looked at each other with blank expressions. Neither one of us had the slightest idea what the answer was. What did it signify?

We received a wonderful answer from Jeff Kanipe, an associate editor at *Astronomy*. His answer is complicated but clear, clearer than we could rephrase. So Jeff generously has consented to let us quote him in full:

The first day of winter and summer depend on when the sun reaches its greatest angular distance north and south of the celestial equator.

Imagine for a moment that the Earth is reduced to a tiny ball floating in the middle of a transparent sphere and that we're on the "outside" looking in. This sphere, upon which the stars seem fixed and around which the moon, planets, and sun seem to move, is called the celestial sphere. If we simply extend the earth's equator to the celestial sphere it forms a great circle in the sky: the celestial equator.

Now imagine that you're back on the Earth looking out toward the celestial sphere. You can almost visualize the celestial equator against the sky. It forms a great arc that rises above the eastern horizon, extends above the southern horizon, and bends back down to the western horizon.

But the sun doesn't move along the celestial

equator. If it did, we'd have one eternal season. Rather, the seasons are caused because the Earth's pole is tilted slightly over 23 degrees from the "straight up" position in the plane of the solar system. Thus, for several months, one hemisphere tilts toward the sun while the other tilts away. The sun's apparent annual path in the sky forms yet another great circle in the sky called the ecliptic, which, not surprisingly, is inclined a little over 23 degrees to the celestial equator.

Motions in the solar system run like clockwork. Astronomers can easily predict (to the minute and second!) when the sun will reach its greatest angular distance north of the celestial equator. This day usually occurs about June 21. If you live in the Northern Hemisphere and note the sun's position at noon on this day, you'll see that it's very high in the sky because it's as far north as it will go. The days are longer and the nights are shorter in the Northern Hemisphere. The sun is thus higher in the sky with respect to our horizon, and remains above the horizon for a longer period than it does during the winter months. Conditions are reversed in the Southern Hemisphere: short days, long nights. It's winter there.

Just reverse the conditions on December 22. In the Northern Hemisphere, the sun has moved as far south as it will go. The days are short, while the lucky folks in the Southern Hemisphere are basking in the long, hot, sunny days.

The first days of spring and fall mark the vernal and autumnal equinox, when the sun crosses the equator traveling north and south. As astronomer Alan M. MacRobert points out, the seasonal divisions are rather arbitrary:

> Because climate conditions change continuously, there is no real reason to have four seasons instead of some other number. Some cultures recognize three: winter, growing, and harvest. When I lived in northern Vermont, people spoke of six: winter, mud, spring, summer, fall, and freezeup.

WHY DO ASTRONOMERS LOOK AT THE SKY UPSIDE DOWN AND REVERSED? WOULDN'T IT BE POSSIBLE TO REARRANGE THE MIRRORS ON TELESCOPES?

Merry Wooten, of the Astronomical League, informs us that most early telescopes didn't yield upside-down images. Galileo's original spyglass used a negative lens as an eyepiece, just as cheap field glasses made with plastic lenses do now. So why do unsophisticated binoculars yield the "proper" image and expensive astronomical telescopes render an "incorrect" one?

Astronomy editor Jeff Kanipe explains:

> The curved light-gathering lens of a telescope bends, or refracts, the light to focus so that light rays that pass through the top of the lens are bent toward the bottom and rays that pass through the bottom of the lens are bent toward the top. The image thus forms upside down and reversed at the focal point, where an eyepiece enlarges the inverted and reversed image.

Alan MacRobert, of *Sky & Telescope* magazine, adds that some telescopes turn the image upside down, and others also mirror-reverse it: "An upside-down 'correct' image can be viewed correctly just by inverting your head. But a mirror image does not become correct no matter how you may twist and turn to look at it."

OK. Fine. We could understand why astronomers live with inverted and upside-down images if they had to, but they don't.

Terrestrial telescopes do rearrange their image. Merry Wooten says that terrestrial telescopes can correct their image by using porro prisms, roof prisms, or most frequently, an erector lens assembly, which is placed in front of the eyepiece to create an erect image.

Why don't astronomical telescopes use erector lenses? For the answer, we return to Jeff Kanipe:

> Most astronomical objects are very faint, which is why telescopes with larger apertures are constantly being proposed: Large lenses and mirrors gather more light than small ones. Astronomers need every scrap of light they can get, and it is for this reason that the image ori-

entation of astronomical telescopes are not corrected. Each glass surface the light ray encounters reflects or absorbs about four percent of the total incoming light. Thus if the light ray encounters four glass components, about sixteen percent of the light is lost. This is a significant amount when you're talking about gathering the precious photons of objects that are thousands of times fainter than the human eye can detect. Introducing an erector into the optical system, though it would terrestrially orient the image, would waste light. We can afford to be wasteful when looking at bright objects on the earth but not at distant, faint galaxies in the universe.

And even if the lost light and added expense of erector prisms weren't a factor, every astronomer we contacted was quick to mention an important point: There IS no up or down in outer space.

Submitted by William DeBuvitz of Bernardsville, New Jersey.

WHY DOES GREASE TURN WHITE WHEN IT COOLS?

You finish frying some chicken. You reach for the used coffee can to discard the hot oil. You open the lid of the coffee can and the congealed grease is thick, not thin, and not the yellowish-gold color of the frying oil you put in before, but whitish, the color of glazed doughnut frosting. Why is the fat more transparent when it is an oil than when it is a grease?

When the oil cools, it changes its physical state, just as transparent water changes into more opaque ice when it freezes. Bill DeBuvitz, a longtime *Imponderables* reader and, more to the point, an associate professor of physics at Middlesex County College in New Jersey, explains:

> When the grease cools, it changes from a liquid to a solid. Because of its molecular structure, it cannot quite form a crystalline structure. Instead, it forms "amorphous regions" and "partial crystals." These irregular areas scatter white light and make the grease appear cloudy.

If grease were to solidify into a pure crystal, it would be much clearer, maybe like glass. Incidentally, paraffins like candle wax behave just like grease: They are clear in the liquid form and cloudy in the solid form.

Submitted by Eric Schmidt of Fairview Park, Ohio.

WHY DOES MENTHOL FEEL COOL TO THE TASTE AND COOL TO THE SKIN?

Of course, the temperature of menthol shaving cream isn't any lower than that of musk shaving cream. So clearly, something funny is going on. R. J. Reynolds's public relations representative, Mary Ann Usrey, explains the physiological shenanigans:

> The interior of the mouth contains many thermo-receptors that respond to cooling. These thermo-receptors may be compared to the receptors for the sensations of "sweet," "salty," "bitter," etc.
>
> In other words, individual receptors respond to specific types of stimulation. For example, a person's perception that sugar is sweet is initiated when the receptors in the mouth for "sweet" are stimulated. Menthol feels cool to the taste because menthol stimulates the thermoreceptors that respond normally to cooling.
>
> Menthol has the ability to "trick" those thermoreceptors into responding. The brain receives the message that what is being experienced is "cool."

Although not as easy to stimulate by menthol as those in the mouth, the skin also contains those types of thermoreceptors, which is why menthol shaving cream or shaving lotion feels cool to the skin.

Submitted by Allan J. Wilke of Cedar Rapids, Iowa.

Heat lightning is actually distant lightning produced by an electrical storm too far away to be seen by the observer. What you see is actually the diffused reflection of the distant lightning on clouds.

You don't hear thunder because the actual lightning is too far away from you for the sound to be audible. There is thunder where the lightning is actually occurring.

WHEN GLASS BREAKS, WHY DON'T THE PIECES FIT BACK TOGETHER PERFECTLY?

We received a wonderful response to this Imponderable from Harold Blake, who you might remember from *When Do Fish Sleep?* as the gentleman who spent some time in college simulating the aroma of Juicy Fruit gum. It's nice to know that Mr. Blake, now a retired engineer, is still trying to find the solutions to the important things in life.

The key point Blake makes about this Imponderable is to remember that while glass appears to be inflexible, it does bend and change shape. If you throw a ball through a plate glass window, the glass will try to accommodate the force thrust upon it; it will bend. But if bent beyond its limits, glass shatters or ruptures.

At the point that the glass breaks, the glass's shape is distorted but the break is a perfect fracture—the parts would fit back together again. But as soon as the glass shatters, the parts begin to minimize their distortion and return to the unstressed state.

When the pieces return to their unstressed state, the fracture is no longer "perfect." Like a human relationship, things are never quite the same after a breakup.

Blake points out that other seemingly inflexible materials show the same tendencies as glass. Ceramics, pottery, and metals, for example, also distort and then return to a slightly altered "original" configuration.

Submitted by Charles Venezia of Iselin, New Jersey.

WHY DOES WOOD "POP" WHEN PUT ON A FIRE?

J ohn A. Pitcher, director of the Hardwood Research Council, was kind enough to tackle this burning Imponderable:

> Wood pops when put on a fire because there are little pockets of sap, pitch [resin], or other volatiles that are contained in the wood. As the wood surface is heated and burns, heat is transferred to the sap or pitch deeper in the wood.
>
> The sap or pitch first liquefies, then vaporizes as the temperature increases. Gasses expand rapidly when heated and put tremendous pressure on the walls of the pitch pocket. When the pressure gets high enough, the pocket walls burst and the characteristic sound is heard.

Submitted by Patric Conroy of Walnut Creek, California.

Of course, "pops" are not unrelated to "crackles." John Pitcher explains that the larger the sap or pitch pockets in the wood, the bigger the pop; but if there are smaller but more numerous pockets, the wood will crackle instead.

The reason fires crackle most when first lit is that the smaller pieces of wood, used as kindling, heat up quickly. The inside sap pockets are penetrated and crackle immediately. Big pieces of wood burn much more slowly, with fewer, intermittent, but louder pops.

For those of you who are, pardon the expression, "would-be" connoisseurs of lumber acoustics, Pitcher provided *Imponderables* readers with a consumer's guide:

> There are distinct differences in the popping characteristics of woods. High on the list of poppers is tamarack or larch. Most conifers are ready poppers. On the other hand, hardwoods,

such as ash, elm, and oak, tend to burn quietly, with only an occasional tastefully subdued pop. You might call them poopers rather than poppers.

Submitted by Andrew F. Garruto of Kinnelon, New Jersey.

Much to our shock, there really is a "who." The International Hydrographic Organization (IHO) is composed of about seventy member countries, exclusively nations that border an ocean (eat your heart out, Switzerland!). Part of their charter is to assure the greatest possible uniformity in nautical charts and documents, including determining the official, standardized ocean boundaries.

All of the oceans of the world are connected to one another—you could theoretically row from the Indian Ocean to the Arctic Ocean (but, boy, would your arms be tired). No one would dispute the borders of the oceans that hit a landmass, but what about the 71 percent of the earth that is covered by sea?

The IHO issues a publication, "Limits of Oceans and Seas," that determines exactly where these water borders are located, but is used more by researchers than sailors. Michel Huet, chief engineer at the International Hydrographic Bureau, the central office of the IHO, wrote to Imponderables and quoted "Limits of Oceans and Seas":

> "The limits proposed...have been drawn up solely for the convenience of National Hydrographic Offices when compiling their Sailing Directions, Notices to Mariners, etc., so as to ensure that all such publications headed with the name of an ocean or sea will deal with the same area, and they are not to be regarded as representing the

result of full geographic study; the bathymetric [depth measurements of the ocean floor] results of various oceanographic expeditions have, however, been taken into consideration so far as possible, and it is therefore hoped that these delimitations will also prove acceptable to oceanographers. These limits have no political significance whatsoever." Therefore, the boundaries are established by common usage and technical considerations as agreed to by the Member States of the IHO.

Essentially, a committee of maritime nations determines the borders and titles for the oceans.

How would the IHO decide on the border between the Atlantic and Pacific? A somewhat arbitrary man-drawn line was agreed upon that extends from Cape Horn, on the southern tip of South America, across the Drake Passage to Antarctica. A specific longitude was chosen, so the border goes exactly north-south from the cape to Antarctica.

Of course, there are no YOU ARE LEAVING THE PACIFIC OCEAN, WELCOME TO THE ATLANTIC OCEAN signs posted along the longitude. But a sailor with decent navigational equipment could determine which ocean he was in—likewise with the boundaries between other oceans.

Unlike the United Nations, most of the time the IHO does not become embroiled in political disputes, presumably because the precise location of the oceans' borders has no commercial or military implications. Disputes are not unheard of, though. For example, Korea and Japan recently tussled about the designation of the sea that divides their countries. Traditionally, the body of water has been called the Sea of Japan, but Korea wanted it changed to "East Sea."

Perhaps we were dozing during some of the year 2000 hoopla, but much to our surprise, the IHO was involved with a rather important event in that year— the debut of a new ocean. The southernmost parts of the Pacific, Atlantic, and Indian oceans (including all the water surrounding Antarctica), up to 60 degrees south, were dubbed the "Southern Ocean." The name was approved by a majority of the IHO and went into effect in 1999, with Australia among the dissenters. Why wasn't this a bigger deal than Y2K?

Submitted by Bonnie Wootten of Nanaimo, British Columbia. Thanks also to Terry Garland, via the Internet.

The liquid found in weather thermometers is usually alcohol with red coloring. The main reason why alcohol is preferred over mercury for weather thermometers is that it is much, much cheaper. And alcohol is superior to water because alcohol is far hardier—it won't freeze even at temperatures well below -40° Fahrenheit.

Why the red additive in weather thermometers? So that you can read it more easily. If weather thermometers used a liquid the color of mercury, you'd have to take the thermometer off the wall to be able to read it.

Since the advantages of alcohol are so apparent, why don't medical thermometers, notoriously difficult to read, contain red-colored alcohol instead of dingy mercury? Despite its greater cost, mercury is prized for its greater expansion coefficient—that is, it expands much more than alcohol or water when subjected to small increases in temperature. A weather thermometer might measure temperatures between -30° and 120° Fahrenheit, a span of 150°, while a medical thermometer might cover only a 10- to 12° range. A doctor might want to know your temperature to the nearest tenth of a degree; if a liquid with a small expansion coefficient were used, you would need a thermometer the length of a base-ball bat to attain the proper degree of sensitivity. We don't know about you, but we'll stick with the stick thermometer.

Couldn't the medical thermometer manufacturers color mercury, then? Actually, they could, but don't, for reasons that Michael A. DiBiasi, of Becton Dickinson Consumer Products, explains:

> When you produce medical instruments, the rule of the road states that the fewer additives that you incorporate into any device or component material, the better off you are in gaining approval to market the device, and in avoiding product recalls that may be tied in to those additives. So fever thermometers use mercury in its natural silver-white color, and the glass tube is usually silk-screened with a background color to make it easier to see the mercury level.

Submitted by Herbert Kraut of Forest Hills, New York.

Even if our hands and hair are already wet, we can't seem to get a healthy lather on the first try when we shampoo our hair. But after we rinse, the shampoo foams up like crazy. Why is lather more luxuriant the second time around?

Evidently, it's because we have greasy hair, according to Dr. John E. Corbett, vice president of technology at Clairol:

> In the first shampoo application, the lather is suppressed by the oils in the hair. When the oils are rinsed off [by the first application], the shampoo lathers much better on the second application.

Submitted by Joe Schwartz of Troy, New York.

Even cigarettes without filters don't burn quickly. If the shredded tobacco is packed tightly enough, not enough oxygen is available to feed the combustion process. The degree of porosity of the paper surrounding the tobacco rod can also regulate the degree of burn.

On a filter cigarette, however, an extra impediment is placed on the combustion process; luckily, it is not asbestos. Mary Ann Usrey, of R. J. Reynolds, explains:

> The filter is attached to the tobacco rod by a special "tipping" paper which is essentially nonporous. This paper acts to extinguish the burning coal by significantly reducing the available oxygen. So, in effect, there is a barrier between the tobacco and the filter, but it is around the cigarette, not actually between the tobacco and the filter in the interior of the cigarette.
>
> Submitted by Frank H. Anderson of Prince George, Virginia.

Most of the salt in the ocean is there because of the processes of dissolving and leaching from the solid earth over hundreds of millions of years, according to Dr. Eugene C. LaFond, president of LaFond Oceanic Consultants. Rivers take the salt out of rocks and carry them into oceans; these eroded rocks supply the largest portion of salt in the ocean.

But other natural phenomena contribute to the mineral load in the oceans. Salty volcanic rock washes into them. Volcanos also release salty "juvenile water," water that has never existed before in the form of liquid. Fresh basalt flows up from a giant rift that runs through all the oceans' basins.

With all of these processes dumping salt into the oceans, one might think that the seas would get saturated with sodium chloride, for oceans, like any other body of water, keep evaporating. Ocean spray is continuously released into the air; and the recycled rain fills the rivers, which aids in the leaching of salt from rocks.

Yet, according to the Sea Secrets Information Services of the International Oceanographic Foundation at the University of Miami, the concentration of salts in the ocean has not changed for quite a while—about, oh, 1.5 billion years or so. So how do oceans rid themselves of some of the salt?

First of all, sodium chloride is extremely soluble, so it doesn't tend to get concentrated in certain sections of the ocean. The surface area of the oceans is so large (particularly since all the major oceans are interconnected) that the salt is relatively evenly distributed. Second, some of the ions in the salt leave with the sea spray. Third, some of the salt disappears as adsorbates, in the form of gas liquids sticking to particulate matter that sinks below the surface of the ocean. The fourth and most dramatic way sodium chloride is removed from the ocean is by the large accumulations left in salt flats on ocean coasts, where the water is shallow enough to evaporate.

It has taken so long for the salt to accumulate in the oceans that the amount of salt added and subtracted at any particular time is relatively small.

While the amount of other minerals in the ocean has changed dramatically, the level of salt in the ocean, approximately 3.5 percent, remains constant.

Submitted by Merilee Roy of Bradford, Massachusetts.
Thanks also to Nicole Chastrette of New York, New York;
Bob and Elaine Juhre of Kettle Falls, Washington;
John H. Herman of Beaverton, Oregon;
Matthew Anderson of Forked River, New Jersey;
and Cindy Raymond of Vincentown, New Jersey.

DOES IT EVER REALLY GET
TOO COLD TO SNOW?

Having withstood a few snowy midwestern winters
in our time, we're not sure we would want to
test this hypothesis personally. Luckily, meteorologists
have.

No, it never gets too cold to snow, but at extremely
low temperatures the amount of snow accumulation
on the ground is likely to be much lower than at 25°
Fahrenheit. According to Raymond E. Falconer, of
the Atmospheric Sciences Research Center, SUNY at
Albany, there is so little water vapor available at sub-
zero temperatures that snow takes the shape of tiny
ice crystals, which have little volume and do not form
deep piles. But at warmer temperatures more water
vapor is available, "so the crystals grow larger and
form snowflakes, which are an agglomerate of ice
crystals." The warmer the temperature is, the larger
the snowflakes become.

What determines the size of the initial snow crystals? It depends upon the distribution of temperature

and moisture from the ground up to the cloud base. If snow forming at a high level drops into much drier air below, the result may be no accumulation whatsoever. In the condition known as "virga," streaks of ice particles fall from the base of a cloud but evaporate completely before hitting the ground.

Submitted by Ronald C. Semone of Washington, D.C.

WHY DOES GRANULATED SUGAR TEND TO CLUMP TOGETHER?

It ain't the heat, it's the humidity. Sugar is hygro-scopic, meaning that it is capable of absorbing moisture from the air and changing its form as a result of the absorption. When sugar is subjected to 80 percent or higher relative humidity, the moisture dissolves a thin film of sugar on the surface of the sugar crystal. Each of these crystals turns into a sugar solution, linked to one another by a "liquid bridge."

According to Jerry Hageney, of the Amstar Corporation, when the relative humidity decreases, "the sugar solution gives up its moisture, causing the sugar to become a crystal again. The crystals joined by the liquid bridge become as one crystal. Thus, hundreds of thousands of crystals become linked together to form a rather solid lump."

Although we can't see the moist film on sugar exposed to high humidity, it won't pour quite as smoothly as sugar that has never been exposed to moisture. But when it dries up again, the liquid bridge is a strong one. Bruce Foster, of Sugar Industry Technologists, told us that the technology used to make sugar cubes utilizes this natural phenomenon.

To make sugar cubes, water is added to sugar in a cube-shaped mold. After the sugar forms into cubes, it is dried out, and voilà! you have a chemical-free way to keep sugar stuck together.

Submitted by Patty Payne of Seattle, Washington.

Rain is water. Water is light in color. Rain clouds are full of water. Therefore, rain clouds should be light. Impeccable logic, but wrong.

Obviously, there are always water particles in clouds. But when the particles of water are small, they reflect light and are perceived as white. When water particles become large enough to form rain-drops, however, they absorb light and appear dark to us below.

Into the flame itself. There are 67 different grades of paraffin, ranging from extremely soft (with low-temperature melting points) to extremely hard (with high-temperature melting points). Conventional candles use paraffin with such low melting points that most will melt in the sun.

Dripless candles use hard paraffin and longer wicks, so that no wax is in direct contact with the flame and so the wax around the wick won't melt or drip.

Submitted by Chuck and Louisa Keighan of Portland, Oregon. Thanks also to Stephen J. Michalak of Myrtle Beach, South Carolina; Mike Hutson of Visalia, California; Richard Roberts of Memphis, Tennessee; and Beth Kennedy of Exeter, New Hampshire.

IF HEAT RISES, WHY DOES ICE FORM ON THE TOP OF WATER IN LAKES AND PONDS?

Anyone who has ever filled an ice-cube tray with water knows that room temperature water decreases in density when it freezes. We also know that heat rises. And that the sun would hit the top of the water more directly than water at the bottom. All three scientific verities would seem to indicate that ice would form at the bottom, rather than the top, of lakes and ponds. "What gives?" demand *Imponderables* readers.

You may not know, however, what Neal P. Rowell, retired professor of physics at the University of South Alabama, told us: Water is most dense at 4° Centigrade (or 39.2° Fahrenheit). This turns out to be the key to the mystery of the rising ice. One of our favorite scientific researchers, Harold Blake, wrote a fine summary of what turns out to be a highly technical answer:

As water cools, it gets more dense. It shrinks. It sinks to the bottom of the pond, lake, rain barrel, wheelbarrow, or dog's water dish. But at 4° Centigrade, a few degrees above freezing, the water has reached its maximum density. It now starts to expand as it gets cooler. The water that is between 4° Centigrade and 0 Centigrade (the freezing point of water) now starts to rise to the surface. It is lighter, less dense.

Now, more heat has to be lost from the water at freezing to form ice at freezing. This is called the "heat of fusion." During the freezing process, ice crystals form and expand to a larger volume, fusing together as they expand, and using more freezing water to "cement" themselves together. The ice crystals are very much lighter and remain on the surface.

Once the surface is frozen over, heat dissipates from the edges and freezing is progressive from the edges. When the unfrozen core finally freezes, there is tremendous pressure exerted from the expansion, and the ice surface or container sides yield, a common annoyance with water pipes.

Once the top layer of the lake or pond freezes, the water below will rarely reach 0° Centigrade; the ice acts effectively as insulation. By keeping the temperature of the water below the ice between 0 and 4° Centigrade, the ice helps some aquatic life survive in the winter when a lake is frozen over.

The strangest element of this ice Imponderable is that since water at 4° Centigrade is at its maximum density, it always expands when it changes temperature, whether it gets hotter or cooler.

Submitted by Richard T. Mitch of Dunlap, California.
Thanks also to Kenneth D. MacDonald of Melrose, Massachusetts;
R. Prickett of Stockton, California;
Brian Steiner of Charlotte, North Carolina;
and John Weisling of Grafton, Wisconsin.

Our correspondent wondered whether this phenomenon was an illusion. Perhaps we are so happy to see the storm flee that the next day, without battering winds, threatening clouds, and endless precipitation, seems beautiful in contrast.

No, it isn't an illusion. Meteorologists call this phenomenon "scavenging." The rainwater that soaks your shoes also cleans away haze and pollutants from the atmosphere and sends it to the ground. At the same time, the wind that wrecks your umbrella during the storm diffuses the irritants that are left in the atmosphere, so that neighbors in surrounding areas aren't subjected to those endless days of boring, pollution-free environments.

Of course, where the pollutants end up depends upon the direction of the prevailing winds. If you are living in a community with generally bad air quality, the wind is your friend anyway. Chances are, the wind is carrying in air from a region with superior air quality.

Submitted by Jack Schwager of Goldens Bridge, New York.

Whips can attain a speed of more than seven hundred miles per hour when snapped, breaking the sound barrier. What you are hearing is a mini sonic boom.

SORRY, SATURN! YOU JUST DON'T HAVE WHAT IT TAKES TO BE A REAL STAR!

What causes a heavenly body to twinkle? Alan MacRobert, of astronomy magazine *Sky & Telescope*, explains:

Twinkling is caused by light rays being diverted slightly—jiggled around—by turbulence where warm and cool air mixes in the upper atmosphere. One moment a ray of light from the star will hit your eye; the next moment, it misses.

Our eyes fool our brains into thinking that the star is jumping around in the sky.

Stars are so far away from us that even when viewed through a sophisticated telescope, they look like single points of light. Even though planets may at first appear the same size as stars to the naked eye, they are actually little disks in the sky. Jeff Kanipe, associate editor of *Astronomy*, told *Imponderables* that "the disks of planets like Venus, Mars, Jupiter, and Saturn can be easily seen by looking at them with a pair of binoculars or a small telescope."

How does this difference in size between stars and planets affect their "twinkling quotient"? We've already established that stars appear to the eye as single points. Kanipe explains how that one point turns into a twinkle:

> When starlight passes through about 200 miles of Earth's atmosphere, the light-bending properties of the different layers of air act like lenses that bend and jiggle the rays to such an extent that the star's position appears to jump about very slightly, causing it to twinkle.

MacRobert contrasts the effect of refraction upon our view of a planet:

> The disk of a planet can be regarded as many points packed close together [yes, like a thousand points of light]. When one point twinkles bright for a moment another may be faint. The differences average out and their combined light appears steady.

Kanipe phrases it a little differently:

> A planet's light comes from every part of its disk, not just a single point. Thus, when the light passes through the atmosphere, the shift in position is smaller than the size of the planet's disk in the sky and the twinkling isn't as pronounced.

Still don't get it? Let's use a more down-to-earth analogy, supplied by Kanipe:

> From the vantage point of a diving board, a dime on the floor of the swimming pool appears to shift violently about because the water acts like a wavy lens that continuously distorts the rays of light coming from the coin. But a submerged patio table, say, looks fairly steady

because the water can't distort the light rays coming from its greater surface area to the point that the table appears to shift out of position.

Submitted by Henry J. Stark of Montgomery, New York.
Thanks also to Frank H. Anderson of Prince George, Virginia,
and J. Leonard Hiebert of Nelson, British Columbia.

What makes you think that clouds aren't dropping? They are. Constantly.

Luckily, cloud drops do not fall at the same velocity as a water balloon. In fact, cloud drops are downright sluggards: They drop at a measly 0.3 centimeters per second. And cloud drops are so tiny, about 0.01 centimeters in diameter, that their descent is not even noticeable to the human eye.

Submitted by Ronald C. Semone of Washington, D.C.

WHAT DOES 0° IN THE FAHRENHEIT SCALE SIGNIFY?

During our school days, we were forced to memorize various points in the Fahrenheit scale. We all know that the freezing point is 32° and that the boiling point is 212°. The normal human body temperature is the inelegantly unround number of 98.6°.

Countries that have adopted the metric system have invariably chosen the Celsius system to measure heat. In the Celsius scale, 0° equals the freezing point.

The Fahrenheit temperature scale was created by a German physicist named Daniel Gabriel Fahrenheit, who invented both the alcohol thermometer and the mercury thermometer. The divisions of his scale aren't quite as arbitrary as they might seem. Zero degrees was chosen to represent the temperature of an equal ice-salt mixture, and 100° was originally supposed to signify the normal body temperature. But Fahrenheit screwed up. Eventually, scientists found that the scale didn't quite work, and the normal body temperature was "down-scaled" to 98.6°.

Submitted by James S. Boczarski, of Amherst, New York.

Although his scale was not based on the freezing and boiling points, Fahrenheit recognized their significance. The interval between the boiling point (212°) and freezing point (32°) numbers exactly 180 degrees on the Fahrenheit scale, a figure with which scientists and mathematicians were used to working.

The increments in a temperature scale have no cosmic significance in themselves. The Celsius system, for example, is less precise than the Fahrenheit in distinguishing slight variations in moderate temperatures. Thus while 180 increments on the Fahrenheit scale are necessary to get from the freezing to the boiling point, the freezing point (0°) on the Celsius scale and the boiling point (100° C) are closer, only 100 increments apart.

In most cases, the meaning of the one-degree increments in temperature scales has more to do with what is intended to be measured by the scale than with any particular mathematical requirements.

The Fahrenheit scale, intended for use in human thermometers, was designed originally to have 100°F represent the normal body temperature. Temperature scales now used by scientists, such as the Kelvin and Rankine scales, use absolute zero (the equivalent of -273.15° C or -459.67° F) as the base point. Rankine uses the same degree increments as Fahrenheit; Kelvin uses the Celsius degree.

Submitted by James L. Foley, of Calabasas, California.

WHY DOES JUST ABOUT EVERYTHING LOOK DARKER WHEN IT GETS WET?

Come to think of it, reader Russell has a point. Drop some water on your new cream-colored blouse and you get a dark spot. Have a clod standing near you spill his Perrier on your navy blue blazer and the light liquid somehow manages to make the coat's dark color even darker. Why is this so?

Elementary physics, it turns out. You lose the true color of the garment in three ways:

1. Even a thin coating of water will force light coming toward the garment to refract within the water film. The available light is thus disbursed.

2. The reflection on the surface of the water itself causes incoherent light scattering.

3. A combination of the two points above ensures that there will be less light available on the surface of the jacket to reflect back to your eyes. Thus the spot will appear darker than the rest of the jacket that doesn't have to compete with water in order to reflect light.

Submitted by Kathleen Russell of Grand Rapids, Michigan. Thanks also to Kent Parks of Raleigh, North Carolina.

**IF ALL TIME ZONES CONVERGE AT
THE NORTH AND SOUTH POLES,
HOW DO THEY TELL TIME THERE?**

Imagine that you are a zoologist stationed at the South Pole. You are studying the nighttime migration patterns of Emperor penguins, which involves long periods observing the creatures. But you realize that while you watch them waddle, you are in danger of missing a very special episode of *The Bachelor* on television unless you set that VCR for the right time. What's a scientist to do?

Well, maybe that scenario doesn't play out too often, but those vertical line markings on globes do reflect the reality. All the time zones do meet at the two poles, and many *Imponderables* readers wonder how the denizens of the South Pole (and the much fewer and usually shorter-term residents of the North Pole) handle the problem.

We assumed that the scientists arbitrarily settled on Greenwich Mean Time (the same time zone where London, England, is situated), as GMT is used as the worldwide standard for setting time. But we found out that the GMT is no more! It is now called UTC (or Coordinated Universal Time—and, yes, we know that the acronym's letter order is mixed up). The UTC is often used at the North Pole as the time standard, and sometimes at the South Pole.

We veered toward the humanities in school partly because the sciences are cut and dried. If there is always a correct answer, then teachers could always determine that we came up with the wrong answer. Science students were subjected to a rigor that we were not.

But when it comes to time zones, the scientists at the poles are downright loosey-goosey: They use whatever time zone they want! We spoke to Charles Early, an engineering information specialist at the Goddard Space Flight Center in Greenbelt, Maryland, who told us that most scientists pick the time zone that is most convenient for their collaborators. For example, most of the flights to Antarctica depart from New Zealand, so the most popular time at the South Pole is New Zealand time. The United States' Palmer Station, located on the Antarctic Peninsula, sets its time according to its most common debarkation site,

Punta Arenas, Chile, which happens to share a time zone with Eastern Standard Time in the United States. The Russian station, Volstok, is coordinated with Moscow time, presumably to ease time-conversion hassles for the comrades back in Mother Russia.

Early researched this subject to answer a question from a child who wondered what time Santa Claus left the North Pole in order to drop off all his presents around the world. Based on our lack of goodies lately, we think Santa has been oversleeping big-time, and now we know that time-zone confusion is no excuse.

Submitted by Thomas J. Cronen of Naugatuck, Connecticut.
Thanks also to Christina Lasley of parts unknown;
Jack Fisch of Deven, Pennsylvania;
Dave Bennett of Fredericton, Ontario;
Paul Keriotis, via the Internet;
Peter Darga of Sterling Heights, Illinois;
Marvin Eisner of Harvard, Illinois;
Jeff Pontious of Coral Springs, Florida;
and Dean Zona, via the Internet.

You think time zones are a problem, how about giving directions to a pal at the South Pole. By definition, every direction would start with "Head north."

In practical terms, though, the distances aren't great at the science stations, and it's not like there are suburbs where you can get lost. But scientists do have a solution to this problem, as Nathan Tift, a meteorologist who worked at the Amundsen-Scott South Pole Station explains:

> If someone does talk about things being north or south here, they are most likely referring to what we call "grid directions," as in grid north and grid south. In the grid system, north is along the prime meridian, or 0 degrees longitude, pointing toward Greenwich, England, south would be 180 longitude, east is 90 degrees, and west is 270 degrees. It's actually quite simple. Meteorologists like myself always describe wind directions using the grid system. It wouldn't mean much to report that the wind at the South Pole always comes from the north!

Submitted by Michael Finger of Memphis, Tennessee.

This isn't the type of question that meteorologists study in graduate school or that receives learned exegeses in scholarly journals, but we got several experts to speculate for us. They came down into two camps.

1. *It ain't the rain, it's the humidity.* Biophysicist Joe Doyle blames the humidity, which rises before rainfall. Of course, humidity itself doesn't smell, but it accentuates the smells of all the objects around it. Everything from garbage to grass smells stronger when it gets damp. Doyle believes that the heightened smell of the flora and fauna around us tips us off subliminally to the feeling that it is going to rain. Richard A. Anthes, president of the University Corporation for Atmospheric Research, points out that many gaseous pollutants also are picked up more by our smell receptors when it is humid.

2. *The ozone did it.* Dr. Keith Seitter, assistant to the executive director of the American Meteorology Association, reminds us that before a thunderstorm, lightning produces ozone, a gas with a distinctive smell. He reports that people who are near lightning recognize the ozone smell (as do those who work with electrical motors, which emit ozone).

Kelly Redmond, meteorologist at the Western Regional Climate Center, in Reno, Nevada, also subscribes to the ozone theory, with one proviso. Ozone emissions are common during thunderstorms in the summer, but not from the rains from stratiform clouds during the cold season. So if it's "smelling like rain" during the winter in Alaska, chances are you are not smelling the ozone at all but the soil, plants, and vegetation you see around you, enhanced by the humidity.

Submitted by Dr. Thomas H. Rich of Melbourne, Victoria, Australia. Thanks also to George Gudz of Prescott, Arizona; Anne Thrall of Pocatello, Idaho; Dr. Allan Wilke of Toledo, Ohio; Matthew Whitfield of Hurdle Mills, North Carolina; Philip Fultz of Twentynine Palms, California; and William Lee of Melville, New York.

WHY DO UNOPENED JARS OF MAYONNAISE, SALAD DRESSING, FRUIT, AND MANY OTHER FOODS STAY FRESH INDEFINITELY ON THE SHELF BUT REQUIRE REFRIGERATION AFTER BEING OPENED?

The three main enemies of freshness in perishable foods are air, heat, and low acidity. Foods such as mayonnaise, salad dressing, and canned fruit all undergo processing to eliminate these hazards. Burton Kallman, director of science and technology for the National Nutritional Foods Association, explains:

> Unopened jars of perishable foods can remain at room temperature because they are sealed with low oxygen levels (sometimes under vacuum), are often sterilized or at least pasteurized, and may contain preservatives which help maintain their freshness.

All three of these foods contain natural ingredients that act as preservatives. Roger E. Coleman, senior vice president of public communications for the

National Food Processors Association, differentiates between foods that must be refrigerated immediately and those that can remain unopened on the shelf:

> Products such as marinated vegetables, salad dressings, and fruits, which contain adequate amounts of added acid ingredients such as vinegar and/or lemon juice, will not support the growth of hazardous microorganisms and only need to be refrigerated after opening to prevent them from spoiling. Other products, such as canned meats and vegetables, do not contain acidic ingredients and, thus, can support the growth of hazardous microorganisms. These products must be refrigerated, not only to retard spoilage but to keep them safe to eat after opening.

This last point is particularly important, for many foods that state "Refrigerate after opening" are perfectly safe to store back on the shelf after they are opened. So why the warning? Barbara Preston, executive director of the Association for Dressings and Sauces, writes:

> Most commercial dressings (with the exception of those bought from a refrigerated display

case) are perfectly safe stored at room temperature. The words 'Refrigerate After Opening' on the label are intended only to help preserve their taste, aroma, and appearance. They do not relate to spoilage. If an already opened jar of salad dressing is accidentally left out for several hours, don't throw it away. There is no danger of spoiling...it just may not taste as fresh.

Submitted by Nancy Schmidt of West New York, New Jersey.

Think of a hurricane as heavyweight boxer Sonny Liston, a powerful force of nature. A building in the face of Liston's onslaught is like George Foreman, strong but anchored to the ground. Without any means of flexibility or escape, the building is a sitting target. A building's massive size offers a greater surface area to the wind, allowing greater total force for the same wind pressure than a tree could offer.

But a tree in a hurricane is like Muhammad Ali doing the rope-a-dope. The tree is going to be hit by the hurricane, but it yields and turns and shuffles its way until the force of the hurricane no longer threatens it. In this case, the metaphor is literal: by bending with the wind, the tree and its leaves can sometimes escape totally unscathed.

Richard A. Anthes, president of the University Corporation for Atmospheric Research, offers another reason why we see so many buildings, and especially so many roofs, blown away during a hurricane.

"Buildings offer a surface which provides a large aerodynamic lift, much as an airplane wing. This lift is often what causes the roof to literally be lifted off the building."

We don't want to leave the impression that trees can laugh off a hurricane. Many get uprooted and are stripped of their leaves. Often we get the wrong impression because photojournalists love to capture ironic shots of buildings torn asunder while Mother Nature, in the form of a solitary, untouched, majestic tree, stands triumphant alongside the carnage.

Submitted by Daniel Marcus of Watertown, Massachusetts.

This Imponderable has been floating around the cosmos for eons and has long been discussed by astronomers, who call it the Moon illusion. Not only the Moon but the Sun appears much larger at the horizon than up in the sky. And constellations, as they ascend in the sky, appear smaller and smaller. Obviously, none of these bodies actually changes size or shape, so why do they seem to grow and shrink?

Although there is not total unanimity on the subject, astronomers, for the most part, are satisfied that three explanations answer this Imponderable. In descending order of importance, they are:

1. As Alan MacRobert of *Sky & Telescope* magazine states it, "The sky itself appears more distant near the horizon than high overhead." In his recent article in *Astronomy* magazine, "Learning the Sky by Degrees," Jim Loudon explains, "Apparently, we perceive the sky not as half a sphere but as half an oblate [flattened at the poles] spheroid—in other words,

the sky overhead seems closer to the observer than the horizon. A celestial object that is perceived as 'projected' onto this distorted sky bowl seems bigger at the horizon." Why? Because the object appears to occupy just as much space at the seemingly faraway horizon as it does in the supposedly closer sky.

2. When reference points are available in the foreground, distant objects appear bigger. If you see the moon rising through the trees, the moon will appear immense, because your brain is unconsciously comparing the size of the object in the foreground (the tree limbs) with the moon in the background. When you see the moon up in the sky, it is set against tiny stars in the background.

Artists often play with distorting perception by moving peripheral objects closer to the foreground. Peter Boyce, of the American Astronomical Society, adds that reference points tend to distort perception most when they are close to us and when the size of the reference points is well known to the observer. We know how large a tree limb is, but our mind plays tricks on us when we try to determine the size of heavenly objects. Loudon states that eleven full moons would fit between the pointer stars of the Big Dipper, a fact we could never determine with our naked eyes alone.

3. The moon illusion may be partially explained by the refraction of our atmosphere magnifying the image. But even the astronomers who mentioned the refraction theory indicated that it could explain only some of the distortion.

A few skeptics, no doubt the same folks who insist that the world is flat and that no astronaut has ever really landed on the Moon, believe that the Moon really is larger at the horizon than when up in the sky. If you want to squelch these skeptics, here are a few counterarguments that the astronomers suggested.

1. Take photos of the Moon or Sun at the horizon and up in the sky. The bodies will appear to be the same size.

2. "Cover" the Moon with a fingertip. Unless your nails grow at an alarming rate, you should be able to cover the Moon just as easily whether it is high or low.

3. Best of all, if you want proof of how easy it is to skew your perception of size, bend over and look at the Moon upside down through your legs. When we are faced with a new vantage point, all reference points and size comparisons are upset, and we realize how much we rely upon experience, rather than our sensory organs, to judge distances and size.

We do, however, suggest that this physically challenging and potentially embarrassing scientific procedure be done in wide-open spaces and with the supervision of a parent or guardian. *Imponderables* cannot be held responsible for the physical or emotional well-being of those in search of astronomical truths.

Submitted by Patrick Chambers, of Grandview, Missouri.

If you, like every other literate human being, have
read the previous entry, then you know why the
Moon looks larger on the horizon than up in the sky,
even though the Moon remains the same size.
Clearly, our eyes can play tricks on us.

Without reference points to guide us, the Moon

doesn't seem to be far away. When you are driving on a highway, the objects closest to your car go whirring by. Barriers dividing the lanes become a blur. You can discern individual houses or trees by the side of the road, but, depending upon your speed, it might be painful to watch them go by. Distant trees and houses move by much more slowly, even though you are driving at the same speed. And distant mountains seem mammoth and motionless. Eventually, as you travel far enough down the highway, you will pass the mountains, and they will appear smaller.

If you think the mountain range off the highway is large or far away, consider the Moon, which is 240,000 miles away and bigger than any mountain range (more than 2,100 miles in diameter). We already know that our eyes are playing tricks with our perception of how big and far away the Moon is. You would have to be traveling awfully far to make the Moon appear to move at all. *Astronomy* editor Jeff Kanipe concludes that without a highway or expanse of landscape to give us reference points "this illusion of nearness coupled with its actual size and distance makes the Moon appear to follow us wherever we go."

This phenomenon, much discussed in physics and astronomy textbooks, is called the parallax and is used to determine how the apparent change in the position of an object or heavenly body may be influenced by the changing position of the observer. Astronomers can determine the distance between a body in space and the observer by measuring the magnitude of the parallax effect.

And then again, Elizabeth, maybe the Moon really is following you.

Submitted by Elizabeth Bogart of Glenview, Illinois.

White light consists of all the primary and secondary colors in the spectrum. Each color is distinguished by the degree to which it scatters and absorbs light. When sunlight hits seawater, part of it is absorbed while the rest is scattered in all directions after colliding with water molecules.

When sunlight hits clear water, red and infrared light absorb rapidly, and blue the least easily. According to Curtiss O. Davis of the California Institute of Technology's Jet Propulsion Laboratory, "only blue-green light can be transmitted into, scattered, and then transmitted back out of the water without being absorbed." By the time the light has reached ten fathoms deep, most of the red has been absorbed.

Why doesn't tap water appear blue? Curtiss continues: "To see this blue effect, the water must be on the order of ten feet deep or deeper. In a glass there is not enough water to absorb much light, not even the red; consequently, the water appears clear."

Thus if clear water is of a depth of more than ten feet, it is likely to appear blue in the sunlight. So how can we explain green and red oceans?

Both are the result not of the optical qualities of sunlight but of the presence of assorted gook in the water itself. A green sea is a combination of the natural blue color with yellow substances in the ocean— humic acids, suspended debris, and living organisms. Red water (usually in coastal areas) is created by an abundance of algae or plankton near the surface of the water. In open waters, comparatively free from debris and the environmental effect of humans, the ocean usually appears to be blue.

Submitted by Jim Albert, of Cary, North Carolina.

Air moves in layers. Often, rain occurs when a higher warm, moist air mass overwhelms a cool, dry air mass at ground level.

Humidity is measured at ground level. When the rain from the higher layer falls through the dry air layer, the humidity on the surface rises, but need not rise to 100 percent. Conversely, when the moist layer is below the high pressure system, the humidity can reach 100 percent on the surface even if the upper air layer is dry.

The conductivity of water is much higher than air. If the water in a swimming pool is colder than body temperature, the water will conduct heat quickly away from our bodies. If it is warmer, such as in a hot tub, the water just as rapidly transfers heat to the body. Differences in temperature in the ambient air transfer heat in the same directions but at a much slower rate.

Richard A. Anthes, president of the University Corporation for Atmospheric Research, emphasized to *Imponderables*: "It is the rate of conduction of heat that we sense as heat or cold."

Submitted by Glenn Worthman of Palo Alto, California.

WHAT IS THE OFFICIAL NAME OF THE MOON?

A long with our correspondent, we've never known what to call our planet's satellite. Moon? The moon? moon? the moon? Dorothy?

We know that other planets have moons. Do they all have names? How do astronomers distinguish one moon from another?

Whenever we have a problem with matters astronomical, we beg our friends at two terrific magazines—*Astronomy* and *Sky & Telescope*—for help. As usual, they took pity on us.

Astronomy's Robert Burnham, like most senior editors, is picky about word usage:

> The proper name of our sole natural satellite is "the Moon" and therefore...it should be capitalized. The 60-odd natural satellites of the other planets, however, are called "moons" (in lower case) because each has been given a proper name, such as Deimos, Amalthea, Hyperion, Miranda, Larissa, or Charon.
>
> Likewise, the proper name for our star is "the Sun" and that for our planet is "Earth" or "the Earth." It's OK, however, to use "earth" in the lower case whenever you use it as a synonym for "dirt" or "ground."

Alan MacRobert, of *Sky & Telescope*, adds that Luna, the Moon's Latin name, is sometimes used in poetry and science fiction, but has never caught on among scientists or the lay public: "Names are used to distinguish things from each other. Since we have only one moon, there's nothing it needs to be distinguished from."

Submitted by A. P. Bahlkow of Sudbury, Massachusetts.

WHAT IN THE HECK IS A TUMBLEWEED? WHY DOES IT TUMBLE? AND HOW CAN IT REPRODUCE IF IT DOESN'T STAY IN ONE PLACE?

Three Imponderables for the price of one. The first part is easy. The most common form of tumbleweed, the one you see wreaking havoc in movie westerns, is the Russian thistle. But actually the term is applied to any plant that rolls with the wind, drops its seed as it tumbles, and possesses panicles (branched flower clusters) that break off.

Usually, the stems of tumbleweed dry up and snap away from their roots in late fall, when the seeds are ripe and the leaves dying. Although tumbleweeds cannot walk or fly on their own, they are configured to move with the wind. The aboveground portion of the thistle is shaped like a flattened globe, so it can roll more easily than other plants.

In his March 1991 *Scientific American* article "Tumbleweed," James Young points out how tumbleweed has adapted to the arid conditions of the Great

Plains. One Russian thistle plant can contain a quarter of a million seeds. Even these impressive amounts of seeds will not reproduce efficiently if dumped all at once. But the flowers, which bloom in the summer, are wedged in the axil between the leaves and the stem, so that their seeds don't fall out as soon as they are subjected to their first tumbles. In effect, the seeds are dispersed sparingly by the natural equivalent of time-release capsules, assuring wide dissemination.

Young points out that tumbleweed actually thrives on solitude. If tumbleweed bumps into another plant, or thick, tall grass, it becomes lodged there, and birds and small animals find and eat the seeds:

> Hence, successful germination, establishment of seedlings, and flowering depend on dispersal to sites where competition is minimal: Russian thistle would rather tumble than fight.

Although songs have romanticized the tumbleweed, do not forget that the last word in "tumbleweed" is "weed." In fact, if the Russian thistle had been discovered in our country in the 1950s rather than in the 1870s, it probably would have been branded a communist plot. Thistle was a major problem for the cowboys and farmers who first encountered it. Although tumbleweed looks "bushy," its leaves are spiny and extremely sharp. Horses were often lacerated by running into tumbleweed in fields and pastures, and the leaves punctured the gloves and pants worn by cowboys.

Tumbleweed has also been a bane to farmers, which explains how tumbleweed spread so fast from the Dakotas down to the Southwest. The seeds of tumbleweed are about the same size as most cereal grains. Farmers had no easy way to separate the thistle seeds from their grains; as "grain" moved through the marketplace, thistle was transported to new "tumbling ground."

Today, tumbleweed's favorite victims are automobiles and the passengers in them. We get into accidents trying to avoid it, trying to outrace it, and from stupid driving mistakes when simply trying to watch tumbleweed tumble.

Submitted by Plácido García of Albuquerque, New Mexico.

We have probably all had this experience. We listen to a tape recording of ourselves talking with some friends. We insist that the tape doesn't sound at all like our voice, but everyone else's sounds reasonably accurate. "Au contraire," the friend retorts. "Yours sounds right, but *I* don't sound like that." According to speech therapist Dr. Mike

D'Asaro, there is a universal pattern of rejection of one's own voice. Is there a medical explanation?

Yes. Speech begins at the larynx, where the vibration emanates. Part of the vibration is conducted through the air—this is what your friends (and the tape recorder) hear when you speak. Another part of the vibration is directed through the fluids and solids of the head. Our inner and middle ears are parts of caverns hollowed out by bone—the hardest bone of the skull. The inner ear contains fluid; the middle ear contains air; and the two are constantly pressing against each other. The larynx is also surrounded by soft tissue full of liquid. Sound transmits differently through the air than through solids and liquids, and this difference accounts for almost all of the tonal differences we hear when reacting negatively to our own voice on a tape recorder.

When we listen to our own voice while we speak, we are not hearing solely with our ears, but also through internal hearing, a mostly liquid transmission through a series of bodily organs. During an electric guitar solo, who hears the "real" sound? The audience, listening to amplified, distorted sound? The guitarist, hearing a combination of the distortion and the predistorted sound? Or would a tape recorder located inside the guitar itself hear the "real" music? The question is moot. There *are* three different sounds being made by the guitarist at any one time, and the principle is the same for the human voice. We can't say that either the tape recorder or the speaker hears the "right" voice, only that the voices are indeed different.

Dr. D'Asaro points out that we have an internal memory of our voice in our brain, and the memory is invariably richer than what we hear in a tape recorder playback. Although there seems to be no consistent pattern in whether folks hear their voices as lower or higher pitched than other listeners, there is no doubt that internal hearing is of much higher fidelity than external hearing. Listening to our own voice on a tape recorder is like listening to a favorite symphony on a bad transistor radio—the sound is recognizable but a pale imitation of the real thing.

After speaking to several agronomists, we can say one thing with certainty: Don't use the word "dirt" casually among soil experts. As Dr. Lee P. Grant of the University of Maryland's Agricultural Engineering Department remonstrated with us, dirt is what one gets on one's clothes or sweeps off the floor. Francis D. Hole, professor emeritus of soil science and geography at the University of Wisconsin-Madison, was a little less gentle:

> What would you do if you were some fine, life-giving soil who is twenty thousand years the senior of the digger, and you were operated on by this fugitive human being with a blunt surgical instrument (but without a soil surgeon's license), and if you were addressed as so much "dirt," to boot? I am suggesting that a self-respecting soil would flee the spot and not be

all there for you to manipulate back into the hole.

So there's the answer: The soil is offended by you calling it dirt, Loren, and has flown the scene of your crime against it.

We promised Grant and Hole we would treat soil with all the respect it was due, and temporarily suppress the use of the "d" word, if they would answer our question. They provided several explanations for why you might run out of soil when refilling a hole:

1. *Not saving all the soil.* Dr. Hole reported one instance, where in their excitement about their work, a team of soil scientists forgot to lay down the traditional canvas to collect the collected soil: "We had lost a lot of the soil in the forest floor, among dead branches and leaves."

2. *You changed the soil structure when you dug up the dirt.* Grant explains:

Soil is composed of organic and inorganic material as well as air spaces and microorganisms. Soil has a structure which includes, among other things, pores (or air spaces) through which water and plant roots pass.

Within the soil are worm, mole, and other tunnels and/or air spaces. All of this structure is destroyed during the digging process.

Hole confirms that stomping on the hole you are refilling can also compact the soil, removing pores and openings, resulting in plugging the hole too tight:

It sounds like a case of poor surgery to me. You treated the patient (the soil) badly by pounding the wound that you made in the first place.

3. *Soil often dries during the digging/handling/moving.* Grant reports that the water in soil sometimes causes the soil to take up more space than it does when dry.

Both of our experts stressed that the scenario outlined by our correspondent is not always true. Sometimes, you may have leftover soil after refilling, as Dr. Hole explains:

It is risky to say that "you never have enough soil to refill." Because sometimes you have too much soil. If you saved all your diggings on a canvas and put it all back, there could be so much soil that it would mound up, looking like a brown morning coffee cake where the hole had been.

...you loosened the soil a lot when you dug it out. When you put the soil back, there were lots of gaps and pore spaces that weren't there before. It might take a year for the soil to settle back into its former state of togetherness. A steady, light rain might speed the process a little bit.

Submitted by Loren A. Larson of Orlando, Florida.

An intriguing Imponderable, we thought, at least until Robert Burnham, editor of *Astronomy*, batted it away with the comment, "Aw, c'mon, you picked an easy one this time!"

Much to our surprise, when astronomers throw lunar fractions around, they are referring to the orbiting cycle of the Moon, not its appearance to us. *Sky & Telescope*'s associate editor, Alan M. MacRobert, explains:

> The Moon is *half* lit when it is a quarter of the way around its orbit. The count begins when the Moon is in the vicinity of the Sun (at "new Moon" phase). "First quarter" is when the Moon has traveled one-quarter of the way around the sky from there. The Moon is full when it is halfway around the sky, and at "third quarter" or "last quarter" when it's three-quarters of the way around its orbit.

Robert Burnham adds that "quarter-Moons" and "half-Moons" aren't the only commonly misnamed lunar apparitions. Laymen often call the crescent moon hanging low in the evening sky a "New Moon," but Burnham points out that at this point, the moon is far from new: "In fact, by then the crescent Moon is some three or four days past the actual moment of New Moon, which is the instant when the center of the Moon passes between the Earth and Sun."

Submitted by Susan Peters of Escondido, California.
Thanks to Gil Gross, of New York, New York.

WHAT PRECISELY IS SEA LEVEL? AND HOW DO THEY DETERMINE EXACTLY WHAT IT IS?

Painstakingly. Obviously, the sea level in any particular location is constantly changing. If you measure the ocean during low tide and then high tide, you won't come up with the same figure. Wind and barometric shifts also affect the elevation of the seas.

But the oceans are joined and their height variation is slight. So geodesists (mathematicians who specialize in the study of measurement) and oceanographers settle for an approximation. Because the cliché that "water seeks its own level" is true, geodesists worry more about sea level variations over time than between places. Measurements are taken all over the globe; there is no one place where sea level is determined. One sea level fits all.

The National Geodetic Survey defines "mean sea level" as the "average location of the interface between ocean and atmosphere, over a period of time sufficiently long so that all random and periodic variations of short duration average to zero." The U.S. National Ocean Service has set 19 as the appropriate number of years to sample sea levels to eliminate such variations; in some cases, measurements are taken on an hourly basis. Geodesists simply add up the 19 years of samples and divide by 19 to arrive at the mean sea level.

The mean sea level has been rising throughout most of the twentieth century—on average, over a millimeter a year. On a few occasions, sea level has risen as much as five or six millimeters in a year, not exactly causing flood conditions, but enough to indicate that the rise was caused by melting of glaciers. If theories of the greenhouse effect and global warming are true, the rise of the global sea level in the future will be more than the proverbial drop in the bucket.

Submitted by Janice Brown of Albany, Oregon.
Thanks also to Wendy Neuman of Plaistow, New Hampshire;
Noel Ludwig of Littleton, Colorado; Jay Howard Horne of Pittsburgh,
Pennsylvania; Charles F. Longaker of Mentor, Ohio;
and Mrs. Violet Wright of Hobbes, New Mexico.

Botany 101. A peanut is not a nut but a legume, closer biologically to a pea or a bean than a walnut or pecan. Each ovary of the plant usually releases one seed per pod, and all normal shells contain more than one ovary.

But not all peanut shells contain two seeds. We are most familiar with Virginia peanuts, which usually contain two but occasionally sprout mutants that feature one, three, or four. Valencia and Spanish peanuts boast three to five seeds per shell.

Traditionally, breeders have chosen to develop two-seeded pods for a practical reason: Two-seeders are much easier to shell. According to Charles Simpson, of Texas A & M's Texas Agricultural Experiment Station, there is little taste difference among the varieties of peanuts, but the three-seed peanuts are quite difficult to shell, requiring tremendous pressure to open without damaging the legume. We do know that patrons of baseball games wouldn't abide the lack of immediate gratification. They'd much rather plop two peanuts than three into their mouths, at least if it means less toil and more beer consumption.

Submitted by Thad Seaver, A Company, 127 FSB.

If there is any radio show that we fear appearing on, it's Ira Fistel's radio show in Los Angeles. Fistel, a lawyer by training, has an encyclopedic knowledge of history, railroad lore, sports, radio, and just about every other subject his audience questions him about, and is as likely as we are to answer an Imponderable from a caller. Fistel can make a *Jeopardy! Tournament of Champions* winner look like a know-nothing.

So when we received this Imponderable on his show and we proceeded to stare at each other and shrug our shoulders (not particularly compelling radio, we might add), we knew this was a true Imponderable. We vowed to find an answer for the next book (and then go back on Fistel's show and gloat about it).

Robert Burnham, senior editor of *Astronomy*, was

generous enough to send a fascinating explanation:

Even the biggest lakes are too small to have tides. Ponds or lakes (even large ones like the Great Lakes) have no tides because these bodies of water are raised all at once, along with the land underneath the lake, by the gravitational pull of the Moon. (The solid Earth swells a maximum of about eighteen inches under the Moon's tidal pull, but the effect is imperceptible because we have nothing that isn't also moving by which to gauge the uplift.)

In addition, ponds and lakes are not openly connected to a larger supply of water located elsewhere on the globe, which could supply extra water to them to make a tidal bulge. The seas, on the other hand, have tides because the water in them can flow freely throughout the world's ocean basins....

On the side of Earth nearest the Moon, the Moon's gravity pulls seawater away from the planet, thus raising a bulge called high tide. At the same time on the other side of the planet, the Moon's gravity is pulling *Earth* away from the *water*, thus creating a second high-tide bulge.

Low tides occur in between because these

are the regions from which water has drained to flow into the two high-tide bulges. (The Sun exerts a tidal effect of its own, but only 46 percent as strong as the Moon's.)

Some landlocked portions of the ocean—the Mediterranean or the Baltic—can mimic the tideless behavior of a lake, although for different reasons. The Mediterranean Sea, for example, has a tidal range measuring just a couple of inches because it is a basin with only a small inlet (the Strait of Gibraltar) connecting it to the global ocean. The Gibraltar Strait is both narrow and shallow, which prevents the rapid twice-a-day flow of immense volumes of water necessary to create a pronounced tide. Thus the rise and fall of the tide in the Atlantic attempts to fill or drain the Med, but the tidal bulge always moves on before very much water can pour in or out past Gibraltar.

Alan MacRobert, of *Sky & Telescope*, summarizes that a body of water needs a large area to slosh around in before tidal effects are substantial, and he provides a simple analogy:

> Imagine a tray full of dirt dotted with thimbles of water, representing a landmass with lakes. You

could tilt it slightly and nothing much would happen. Now imagine a tray full of water—an ocean. If you tilted it just a little, water would sloop out over your hands.

Submitted by a caller on the Ira Fistel show,
KABC-AM, Los Angeles, California.

WHAT KIND OF CONTAINER HOLDS THE RAIN MEASURED BY METEOROLOGISTS?

You can set a bucket outside in your backyard, let the precipitation accumulate, and measure the bucket with a ruler. But after a while the thought is likely to occur to you: How big is the container supposed to be? Sure, it will take more rain to fill an inch of a big bucket than a thin beaker, but then the larger circumference of the bucket will also trap more water. Hmmmm. This isn't as simple as it first seemed.

It turns out that meteorologists don't let this stuff worry them too much. They use many different devices to measure rainfall. Perhaps the most common is the eight-inch rain gauge, a simple metal cylinder with an eight-inch-diameter top. The water is funneled from the outside cylinder into a smaller inner gauge. The water in the inner gauge is measured by a calibrated wooden or metal stick (which can convert the contents of different-sized gauges into the "inches" we hear about in weather reports). By funneling the water into the narrow inner gauge, the vertical scale is expanded, allowing accurate reading of rainfall to the nearest hundredth of an inch.

Richard Williams, meteorologist for the National Weather Service, told *Imponderables* that most of his agency's offices use another method: weighing rain in a bucket and using a mathematical formula to convert weight into hundredths.

Williams adds that in a third type of gauge, rainfall is not collected at all:

> As it falls, each one-hundredth inch of precipitation fills a small metal "bucket." The bucket fills, tips over, and then empties. Each fill/empty cycle triggers an electrical contact and the number of "tips" is charted to determine the rainfall. This is particularly useful in determining the rate of rainfall and in making a permanent chart of the event.

Other variables affect accurate measurement of rainfall. But the most important problem is wind. Ground-level gauges will collect more rain, and tend to be more accurate, than those aboveground, especially if accompanied by an antisplash grid. If the rain gauge is set above the ground, high winds can create uneven distribution of rain and splashing of water onto, rather than into, the gauge.

The problems in measuring rainfall are minor compared to measuring snowfall. Wind is a particular problem since blowing snow, rather than falling snow, might accumulate in gauges, particularly ground-level gauges. The temperature when the snow was formed, wind patterns, and how long the snow has been caught in the gauge may determine whether snow accumulates in air-filled, feathery layers or is compacted down to a tight, dense pack. Since the density of fallen snow varies tremendously, scientists require some way to compare snowfalls accumulated under different conditions.

Meteorologists use several techniques to deal with these problems:

1. **Snow boards.** These boards are put out on the ground. The accumulation is measured on an hourly basis and then cleaned off. This labor-intensive method assures a reading before the snow can pack down. But any one board might not be representative of an area, so many must be used if an accurate assessment of precipitation is important.

2. **Weighing.** Essentially the same technique we discussed with rain gauges. A heating element is put into a gauge (often a standard rain gauge) so that the snow melts. The water is then weighed and converted into "inches."

3. **Snow pillows.** These immediately record the weight of the snow that accumulates above them without converting the snow into water.

Submitted by Ted Roter of Los Angeles, California.
Thanks also to Valerie M. Shields of Danville, California.

WHY ARE CITIES WARMER THAN THEIR OUTLYING AREAS?

In almost every metropolitan area in the United States and Canada, the city is warmer than its immediately surrounding areas. Compared to suburban and rural areas, cities have gotten warmer throughout the twentieth century.

Do the cities themselves generate enough heat to raise the temperature measurably? Is there something about cities that allows them to retain heat? The answer to both questions: Yes.

The heat generated by buildings, factories, vehicles, lighting, and other by-products of modern technology is enough to raise the temperature a degree or two in densely populated cities. The hot air exhaled by air conditioners during summer months affects the temperature outside as surely, if less dramatically, as it affects the temperature inside an air-conditioned room.

But even if cities did not generate their own heat, they would still be warmer than rural or suburban areas. When the sun shines on the flat, featureless Kansas countryside, the light is reflected back to the sky. When the sun shines in midtown Manhattan, the light bounces from skyscraper to skyscraper like a manic Ping-Pong ball—more of the sun's warmth lingers close to ground level than on the Kansan farm and more warmth is absorbed in the city. In fact, buildings and cement pavements can retain more heat and more sunlight than grass, trees, or the farmer's topsoil.

Precipitation has a cooling effect in the country. Rain is stored in the ground and recycles itself through evaporation and plant respiration, thus absorbing heat. In the city, precipitation is funneled into sewers, effectively eliminating much of its cooling effect. The relative lack of this evaporation in the city explains why cities tend to be less humid than rural areas.

It is commonly assumed that air pollution is what makes cities warmer. Since dust particles can absorb radiation, the theory goes, the more polluted the city, the higher the temperature is artificially raised. There is only one problem with this hypothesis: Dust particles can also *reflect* radiation, bouncing rays that would otherwise be trapped near ground level back up to the sky. The jury is still out on the net effects of pollution on temperature.

One fact remains indisputable, though. On extremely windy days, the temperature differences between city and country tend to disappear; on calm days, there is more of a discrepancy than normal. The wind mitigates human intrusion upon the "natural" climate.

While modern life hasn't seemed to affect wind patterns, we have already created a lifestyle that might permanently change our temperature patterns, at least in metropolitan areas. Meteorologists have little idea, at this point, if these barely perceptible changes (cities have become a few degrees warmer in the last fifty years or so) will create profound changes in our ecosystem. They might. And we could usher in the next Ice Age with our cities as hothouses.

WHY DO PEOPLE LOOK UP WHEN THINKING?

Medical doctors have a nasty habit. You pose them a particularly tough Imponderable and they answer, "I don't know." Most medical and scientific research is done on topics that seem likely to yield results that can actually help clinicians with everyday problems. Determining why people look up when thinking doesn't seem to be a matter of earth-shattering priority.

Ironically, some serious psychologists *have* decided that this question is important, have found what they think is a solution to the Imponderable and, most amazingly, found a very practical application for this information. These psychologists are known as neurolinguists.

Neurolinguists believe that many of our problems in human interaction stem from listeners not understanding the frame of reference of the people speaking to them. Neurolinguists have found that most people tend to view life largely through one dominant sense—usually sight, hearing, or touching. There are many clues to the sensory orientation of a person, the most obvious being his or her choice of words in explaining thoughts and feelings. Two people with varying sensory orientations might use totally different verbs, adjectives, and adverbs to describe exactly the same meaning. For example, a hearing-oriented person might say, "I hear what you're saying, but I don't like the sound of your voice." The visually oriented person might say, "I see what you mean, but I think your real attitude is crystal clear." The touch-dominant person (neurolinguists call them kinesthetics) would be more likely to say, "I feel good about what you are saying, but your words seem out of touch with your real attitude."

Neurolinguistically trained psychologists have found that they can better understand and assist clients once they have determined the client's dominant sense (what they call the client's representational system). All three of the above quotes meant the same thing: "I understand you, but your words belie your true emotions." Neurolinguists adapt their choice of words to the representational system of the client, and they have found that it has been a boon to establishing client trust and to creating a verbal shorthand between psychologist and patient. Any feeling that can be expressed visually can be expressed kinesthetically or auditorily as well, so the psychologist merely comes to the patient rather than having the patient come to the psychologist—it helps eliminate language itself as a barrier to communication.

When grappling with finding the answer to a question, most people use one of the three dominant senses to seek the solution. If you ask people what their home phone number was when they were twelve years old, three different people might use the three different dominant senses of vision, hearing, and feeling. One might try to picture an image of the phone dial; one might try to remember the sound of the seven digits, as learned by rote as a small child; and the last may try to recall the feeling of dialing that phone number. Notice that all three people were trying to remember an image, sound, or feeling from the past. But some thoughts involve creating new images, sounds, or feelings. Neurolinguists found they could determine both the operative representational system of their clients and whether they were constructing new images or remembering old ones before the clients even opened their mouths—by observing their eye movements.

These eye movements have now been codified. There are seven basic types of eye movements, each of which corresponds to the use of a particular sensory apparatus. Please note that these "visual accessing cues" are for the average right-handed person; left-handers' eyes ordinarily move to the opposite side. Also, "left-right" designations indicate the direction from the point of view of the observer.

Direction	Thought Process
up-right	visually remembered images
up-left	visually constructing [new] images
straight-right	auditory remembered sounds or words
straight-left	auditory constructed [new] sounds or words
down-right	auditory sounds or words (often what is called an "inner dialogue")
down-left	kinesthetic feelings (which can include smell or taste)

There is one more type of movement, or better, non-movement. You may ask someone a question and he will look straight ahead with no movement and with eyes glazed and defocused. This means that he is visually accessing information.

Try this on your friends. It works. There *are* more exceptions and complications, and this is an admittedly simplistic summary of the neurolinguists' methodology. For example, if you ask someone to describe his first bicycle, you would expect an upward-right movement as the person tries to remember how the bike looked. If, however, the person imagines the bike as sitting in the bowling alley where you are now sitting, the eyes might move up-left, as your friend is constructing a new image with an old object. The best way to find out is to ask your friend how he tried to conjure up the answer.

Neurolinguistics is still a new and largely untested field, but it is fascinating. Most of the information in this chapter was borrowed from the work of Richard Bandler and John Grinder. If you'd like to learn more about the subject, we'd recommend their book *frogs into Princes* (sic).

To get back to the original Imponderable—why do people tend to look up when thinking? The answer seems to be, and it is confirmed by our experiments with friends, that most of us, a good part of the time, try to answer questions by visualizing the answers.

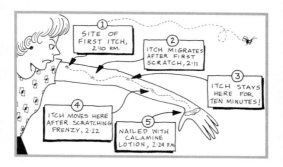

The short answer is: We don't know.

Here's the long answer. Itching is an enigmatic phenomenon. If a patient complains to a doctor that she has horrible itching and the doctor finds hives on the surface of the skin, the doctor can treat the growth and alleviate the itching symptoms. But much itching has no obvious cause and is not associated with any accompanying illness. Scientists can induce itching by heating the skin too close to the pain threshold or giving subjects certain chemicals, especially histamines (thus explaining why doctors prescribe antihistamines as a treatment for itching), but the ability to induce itching -doesn't mean that doctors know its etiology.

This much is known. There are sensory receptors just below the surface of the skin that send messages to the brain. The itch sensation seems to flow along the same pathways of the nervous system as pain sensations. According to Dr. George F. Odland, professor of dermatology at the University of Washington Medical School, the vast majority of sensory receptors are "free" nerve terminals. These "free" terminals do not seem to be designed for any specialized or particular function, but they carry both pain and itch sensations to the brain. These pain receptors are the most common in our nervous systems. When they operate at a low level of activity, they seem to signal itchiness rather than pain.

Many scientists have speculated about the function of itching. Some believe that itching exists in order to warn us of impending pain if action is not taken. Others speculate about the usefulness of itching in letting primitive man know it was time to pluck the vermin and maggots out of his skin and hair. Itchiness can also be an early symptom of more serious illnesses, including diabetes and Hodgkin's disease.

Itching sensations are distinct from ticklishness, which at least some people find pleasurable. Itching is rarely pleasurable; in fact, most people tolerate itching less well than pain. Patients with severe itching are invariably more than willing to break the skin, inducing pain and bleeding, in order to remove the itch.

WHAT IS THE DIFFERENCE BETWEEN A "MOUNTAIN" AND A "HILL"?

Although we think you are making a mountain out of a molehill, we'll answer this Imponderable anyway. Most American geographers refer to a hill as a natural elevation that is smaller than 1,000 feet.

Anything above 1,000 feet is usually called a mountain. In Great Britain, the traditional boundary line between hill and mountain is 2,000 feet.

Still, some geographers are not satisfied with this definition. "Hill" conjures up rolling terrain; "mountains" connote abrupt, peaked structures. A mound that rises two feet above the surrounding earth may attain an elevation of 8,000 feet, if it happens to be located in the middle of the Rockies, whereas a 999-foot elevation, starting from a sea-level base, will appear massive. For this reason, most geographers feel that "mountain" may be used for elevations under 1,000 feet if they rise abruptly from the surrounding terrain.

The *Oxford English Dictionary* states that "hill" may also refer to nonnatural formations, such as sand heaps, mounds, or, indeed, molehills.

Submitted by Thomas J. Schoeck of Slingerlands, New York. Thanks also to F. S. Sewell of San Jose, California.

We like to think of a home as a bulwark, a refuge from the vicissitudes and capriciousness of the outside world. The infrastructure of a house consists of elements like beams, pillars, and foundations, words that connote steadiness, permanence, and immutability.

But architects we talked to soon disabused us of this notion. In fact, talking to an architect about the stability of houses is a little like talking to Norman Bates about shower safety. In particular, we were startled by a book called *How Buildings Work: The Natural Order of Architecture*, written by Edward Allen, and passed on to us by James Cramer, executive vice president/CEO of the American Institute of Architects. In one chapter, "Providing for Building Movement," Allen details the many ways in which buildings move, and if we weren't averse to clichés and bad puns, we would say that the opening rocked us to our very foundations:

A building, even a seemingly solid, massive one, is never at rest. Its motions are usually very small ones, undetectable by the unaided eye, but most of them are of virtually irresistible force, and would tear the building to pieces if not provided for in some way.

Allen states that in an average house, all of these components can and do move:

1. The soil underneath the foundation buckles under the weight of the new foundation.

2. Materials that are put in place while wet,

such as mortar, concrete, and lime plaster, shrink as they harden.

3. Some dry materials, such as gypsum plaster, tend to expand and push against adjoining elements.

4. Most lumber used in houses is not completely dry when put in place. Wet lumber shrinks.

5. Structural elements that carry weight loads, such as beams, pillars, and columns, deflect under the weight.

6. Wind and earthquakes cause more "natural" deflection.

7. Wood and concrete sag.

8. Wood, in particular, tends to expand when exposed to high humidity and contract in dry conditions. When humidity decreases noticeably, such as when heat is put on to warm a room in winter, the wood creaks noticeably.

9. Any material adjoining another material with different movement characteristics is in danger of scraping against another or moving away from the other, which can cause movement and noise.

10. All of the above movements can and do cause noise, but the most common noise associated with "settling" is the actual expansion and contraction of the building. Allen explains:

Back-and-forth movements caused by thermal and moisture effects occur constantly. A building grows measurably larger in warm weather, and smaller in cold weather. A roof, heated by the sun, grows larger in the middle of the day while the cooler walls below stay the same size. At night the roof cools and shrinks.

And so on and so on. The architect's planning compensates for the inevitable movement of these materials. Or at least we hope that it does. Otherwise, the creaking noises might lead us to the same fate as Janet Leigh's in *Psycho*.

Submitted by Joanne Walker of Ashland, Massachusetts.
Thanks also to Dr. Emil S. Dickstein of Youngstown, Ohio.

WHY DO SOME ICE CUBES COME OUT CLOUDY AND OTHERS COME OUT CLEAR?

A caller on the Merle Pollis radio show, in Cleveland, Ohio, first confronted us with this problem. We admitted we weren't sure about the answer, but subsequent callers all had strong convictions about the matter. The only problem was that they all had *different* convictions.

One caller insisted that the mineral content of the water determined the opacity of the cube, but this theory doesn't explain why all the cubes from the same water source don't come out either cloudy or clear.

Two callers insisted that the temperature of the water when put into the freezer was the critical factor. Unfortunately, they couldn't agree about whether it was the hot water or the cold water that yielded clear ice.

We finally decided to go to an expert who confirmed what we expected—all the callers were wrong. Dr. John Hallet, of the Atmospheric Ice Laboratory of the Desert Research Institute in Reno, Nevada, informed us that the key factor in cloud formation is the temperature of the freezer.

When ice forms slowly, it tends to freeze first at one edge. Air bubbles found in a solution in the water have time to rise and escape. The result is clear ice cubes.

The clouds in ice cubes are the result of air bubbles formed as ice is freezing. When water freezes rapidly, freezing starts at more than one end, and water residuals are trapped in the middle of the cube, preventing bubble loss. The trapped bubbles make the cube appear cloudy.

WHAT'S THE DIFFERENCE BETWEEN A LAKE AND A POND?

This is an Imponderable?" we hear you muttering beneath your breath as you read the question. "A lake is a big pond."

Sure, you're right. But have you considered exactly what is the dividing line in size between a lake and a pond? And what separates a lake from a sea or a pool? Do you think you know the answer?

Well, if you do, why don't you go into the field of geography or topography or geology? Because the professionals in these fields sure don't have any standard definitions for any of these bodies of water.

As stated in the past *National Mapping Division's Topographic Instructions'* "Glossary of Names for Topographic Forms," a lake is "Any standing body of inland water generally of considerable size." The same publication classifies a pond as "a small freshwater lake." But other government sources indicate that saltwater pools may be called lakes.

And absolutely no one is willing to say what the

dividing line in size is between the lake and the pond. In fact, the only absolutely clear-cut distinction between the two is that a lake is always a natural formation; if it is man-made, the body is classified as a pond. Ponds are often created by farmers to provide water for livestock. Some ponds are created to provide feeding and nesting grounds for waterfowl. Hatcheries create stocked ponds to breed fish.

Many communities try to inflate the importance of their small reservoirs by calling them lakes rather than ponds. No one is about to stop them.

Submitted by Jeffrey Chavez of Torrance, California.
Thanks also to Ray Kerr of Baldwin, Missouri,
and Eugene Bender of Mary, Missouri.

WHAT'S THE DIFFERENCE BETWEEN
AN OCEAN AND A SEA?

The same folks who are having trouble distinguishing between lakes and ponds are struggling
with this one, too. Once again, there is general agree-
ment that an ocean is larger than a sea.

The standard definition of an ocean, as stated in
the United States Geological Survey's Geographic
Names Information Service, is "The great body of
saltwater that occupies two-thirds of the surface of
the earth, or one of its major subdivisions." Notice
the weasel words at the end. Is the Red Sea a "major
subdivision" of the Indian Ocean? If so, why isn't it
the Red Ocean? Or simply referred to as the Indian
Ocean?

Most but by no means all seas are almost totally
landlocked and connected to an ocean or a larger
sea, but no definition we encountered stated this as a
requirement for the classification. Geographical and
geological authorities can't even agree on whether a
sea must always be saline: the United States

Geological Survey's Topographical Instructions say yes; but in their book *Water and Water Use Terminology*, Professors J. O. Veatch and C. R. Humphrys indicate that "sea" is sometimes used interchangeably with "ocean":

> In one place a large body of salt water may be called lake, in another a sea. The Great Lakes, Lake Superior and others, are freshwater but by legal definition are *seas*.

The nasty truth is that you can get away with calling most places whatever names you want. We often get asked what the difference is between a "street" and an "avenue" or a "boulevard." At one time, there were distinctions among these classifications: A street was a paved path. "Street" was a useful term because it distinguished a street from a road, which was often unpaved. An avenue was, in England, originally a roadway leading from the main road to an estate, and the avenue was always lined with trees. Boulevards were also tree-lined but were much wider thoroughfares than avenues.

Most of these distinctions have been lost in practice over the years. Developers of housing projects have found that using "street" to describe the roadways in their communities makes them sound drab and plebeian. By using "lane," which originally referred to a narrow, usually rural road, they can conjure up Mayberry rather than urban sprawl. By using "boulevard," a potential buyer visualizes Paris rather than Peoria.

For whatever reason, North Americans seem to like lakes more than seas. We are surrounded by oceans to the west and east. By standard definitions, we could certainly refer to Lake Ontario, which is connected, via the St. Lawrence, to the Atlantic, as the Ontario Sea. But we don't. And no one, other than *Imponderables* readers, evidently, is losing any sleep over it.

Submitted by Don and Marian Boxer of Toronto, Ontario.
Thanks also to June Puchy of Lyndhurst, Ohio.

The definitions are easy. A sunrise is defined as occurring when the top of the sun appears on a sea-level horizon. A sunset occurs when the top of the sun goes just below the sea-level horizon.

But how do scientists determine the times? No, they do not send meteorologists out on a ladder and have them crane their necks. No observation is involved at all—just math. By crunching the numbers based on the orbit of the Earth around the Sun, the sunrise and sunset times can be calculated long in advance.

Richard Williams, a meteorologist at the National Weather Service, explains that published times are only approximations of what we observe with our naked eyes:

The time of sunrise and sunset varies with day

of the year, latitude, and longitude. The published sunrise and sunset times are calculated without regard to surrounding terrain. That is, all computations are made for a sea-level horizon, even in mountainous areas. Thus the actual time of sunrise at a particular location may vary considerably from the "official" time.

When we observe sunset, the Sun has already gone below the horizon. The Earth's atmosphere "bends" the Sun's rays and delays the sunset by about three minutes. Likewise with sunrise, the sun makes its first appearance before it would on a planet with no atmosphere. We actually get five to ten minutes of extra sunlight due to this effect.

Submitted by a caller on the Larry Mantle Show,
Pasadena, California.

With the help of Richard A. Anthes, president of the University Corporation for Atmospheric Research, we can lay out the answer to this

Imponderable with a logical precision that Mr. Wizard would admire.

1. Static electricity relies upon the buildup of an electrical charge difference between two objects and the sudden release of this difference in an electrical spark.

2. In order to build up a charge difference sufficient to create static electricity, there should not be much electrical conductivity in the air.

3. The conductivity of moist air is greater than the conductivity of dry air.

4. Relative humidity inside houses or other buildings is usually much lower in the winter than the summer.

5. Therefore, static electricity is more likely to occur in the winter than in the summer.

Static electricity can occur in the summer if the humidity happens to be low that day or if air conditioning dehumidifies the air inside.

Submitted by Reverend Ken Vogler of Jeffersonville, Indiana.

WHY DON'T TREES ON A SLOPE GROW PERPENDICULAR TO THE GROUND AS THEY DO ON A LEVEL SURFACE?

Trees don't give a darn if they're planted on a steep hill in San Francisco or a level field in Kansas. Either way, they'll still try to reach up toward the sky and seek as much light as possible.

Botanist Bruce Kershner told Imponderables that

this strong growth preference is based on the most important of motivations: survival. Scientifically, this is called "phototropism," or the growth of living cells toward the greatest source of light. Light provides trees with the energy and food that enable them to grow in the first place.

There is also another tropism (involuntary movement toward or away from a stimulus) at work—geotropism—the movement away from the pull of gravity (roots, unlike the rest of the tree, grow toward the gravitational pull). Even on a hill slope, the pull of gravity is directly down, and the greatest source of average light is directly up. In a forest, the source of light is only up.

There are cases where a tree might not grow directly up. First, there are some trees whose trunks grow outward naturally, but whose tops still tend to point upward. Second, trees growing against an overhanging cliff will grow outward on an angle toward the greatest concentration of light (much like a house plant grows toward the window). Third, it is reported that in a few places on earth with natural geomagnetic distortions (e.g., Oregon Vortex, Gold Hill, Oregon), the trees grow in a contorted fashion. The gravitational force is abnormal but the light source is the same.

John A. Pitcher, of the Hardwood Research Council, adds that trees have developed adaptive mechanisms to react to the sometimes conflicting demands of phototropism and geotropism:

Trees compensate for the pull of gravity and the slope of the ground by forming a special kind of reaction wood. On a slope, conifer trees grow faster on the downhill side, producing compression wood, so named because the wood is pushing the trunk bole uphill to keep it straight. Hardwoods grow faster on the uphill side, forming tension wood that pulls the trunk uphill to keep it straight.

Why softwoods develop compression wood and hardwoods develop tension wood is one of the unsolved mysteries of the plant world.

We'll put that unsolved mystery on our to-do list.

Submitted by Marvin Shapiro of Teaneck, New Jersey.
Thanks also to Herbert Kraut of Forest Hills, New York;
and Gregory Laugle of Huber Heights, Ohio.

Richard Williams, a meteorologist at the National Weather Service's National Severe Storms Forecast Center, has actually paid cash money to buy *Imponderables* books (we knew there was something we like about him), and sent in his own Imponderables in the past. And now he was kind enough to send us a detailed letter on the subject at hand.

Williams emphasizes that it is windier over land as well as lake during midday. However, the wind increase is accentuated over the relatively smooth, open surface of a lake.

Often, the lowest layers of the atmosphere are at rest during the night and more active or turbulent by day. At night, particularly on clear nights, the earth's surface cools along with the adjacent lowest layers of the atmosphere. The lower layers cool faster than the higher layers, producing a "stable" temperature regime with cool air at ground level and relatively warmer air above the surface.

Under these conditions a temperature inversion will form a few hundred feet above the earth's surface. An inversion is a vertical zone in which temperatures rise with increasing altitude versus the normal cooling. The inversion serves as a barrier or boundary—separating the near-surface air from wind flow aloft. Often at night, calm or very light wind flow will occur at ground level even though the winds aloft continue with little change in speed from day to night.

After sunrise, if the day is sunny or at least partially so, the sun warms the ground. In the lowest layers of the atmosphere, warm, turbulent mixing occurs and the inversion boundary disappears. Once this happens, the general wind flow resumes at the surface. Winds that were probably present during the night just a few hundred feet above the surface can again be felt at ground level. *The midday increase in winds is most pronounced over water where there is less resistance to wind flow.*

Another effect occurs along a coastline and over large lakes. Above a large body of water, local land-to-water wind circulations develop due to the unequal heating of water and land surfaces. This differential heating during the afternoon produces a water-to-land breeze, known as the sea breeze or lake breeze. At night a weaker land-to-water low level breeze can occur: the land breeze.

Submitted by C. Loewenson of New York, New York.

A few facts about clouds will give us the tools to answer this question:

1. A warm volume of air at saturation (i.e., 100 percent relative humidity), given the same barometric pressure, will hold more water vapor than a cold volume of air. For example, at 86° Fahrenheit, seven times as much water vapor can be retained as at 32° Fahrenheit.

2. Therefore, when a volume of air cools, its relative humidity increases until it reaches 100 percent relative humidity. This point is called the dew point temperature.

3. When air at dew point temperature is cooled even further, a visible cloud results (and ultimately, precipitation).

4. Therefore, the disappearance of a cloud is caused by the opposite of #3. Raymond E. Falconer, of the Atmospheric Sciences Research Center, explains:

As a volume of air moves downward from lower to higher barometric pressure, it becomes warmer and drier, with lower relative humidity. This causes the cloud to evaporate.

When we see clouds, the air has been rising and cooling with condensation of the invisible water vapor into visible cloud as the air reaches the temperature of the dew point. When a cloud encounters drier air, the cloud droplets evaporate into the drier air, which can hold more water vapor.

When air is forced up over a mountain, it is cooled, and in the process a cloud may form over the higher elevations. However, as the air descends on the lee side of the mountain, the air warms up and dries out, causing the cloud to dissipate. Such a cloud formation is called an orographic cloud.

Submitted by Rev. David Scott of Rochester, New York.

WHY IS THE BARK OF A TREE DARKER THAN THE WOOD INSIDE?

Depends on how and where you slice it. Actually, there is more than one bark in a tree. A living inner bark, called the phloem, is relatively light in color and is composed of the same cells as wood. When the enzymes in phloem are exposed to air, oxidation darkens it, just as a peeled apple or banana discolors when exposed to air.

The outer bark of a tree, called the rhytidome, is dark. Dark and dead. The main purpose of the rhytidome is to protect the inside of the tree, so it contains tannins (acids used in tanning and in medicine), phenols, and waxes, which help form a barrier to protect the tree from invading fungi and insects. These protective substances are the source of the outer bark's dark color. The degree to which the color of outer and inner barks of trees compare to their wood varies considerably, as John A. Pitcher, of the Hardwood Research Council, explains:

The concentration of tannins, waxes, and phenols varies from tree to tree and between species. Tannins are still extracted from bark for use in the leather curing process (e.g., genuine oak-tanned leathers). On the other hand, [lighter-colored] wine bottle corks come from the dead inner bark of the corkbark oak, *Quercus suber*. The bark is nearly the same color as the wood itself.

Submitted by Jill Davies of Forest, Mississippi.

"They," of course, is Du Pont, which owns the registered trademark for Teflon and its younger and now more popular cousin, Silverstone. G. A. Quinn, of Du Pont, told *Imponderables* that the application of both is similar:

> When applying Silverstone to a metal frypan, the interior of the pan is first grit-blasted, then a primer coat is sprayed on and baked. A second layer of Polytetrafluoroethylene (PTFE) is applied, baked and dried again. A third coat of PFTE is applied, baked and dried.
>
> About the only thing that sticks to PTFE is PTFE. So, the 3-coat process used in Silverstone forms an inseparable bond between the PTFE layers and the primer coat bonds to the rough, grit-blasted metal surface.

Du Pont has recently introduced Silverstone Supra, also a three-layer coating that is twice as durable as conventional Silverstone.

Submitted by Anthony Virga, of Yonkers, New York.

WHY DOESN'T GLUE GET
STUCK IN THE BOTTLE?

There are two basic reasons:

1. In order for glue to set and solidify, it must dry out. Latex and water-based glues harden by losing water, either by absorption into a porous substrate (the surface to be bonded) or by evaporation into the air. The glue bottle, at least if it is capped tightly, seals in moisture.

2. Different glues are formulated to adhere to particular substrates. If the glue does not have a chemical adhesion to the substrate, it will not stick. For example, John Anderson, technical manager for Elmer's Laboratory (makers of Elmer's Glue-All), told us that the Elmer's bottle, made of polyethylene, does not provide a good chemical adhesion for the glue.

Even when the cap is left off, and the glue does lose water, the adhesion is still spotty. We can see this effect with the cap of many glue bottles. In most cases, dried glue can and does cake onto the tip after repeated uses. But Anderson points out that the adhesion is "tenuous," and one can easily clean the top while still wet and remove the glue completely. Likewise, if you poured Elmer's on a drinking glass, it might adhere a little, but you could easily wipe it off with a cloth or paper towel, because the glue cannot easily penetrate the "gluee."

Submitted by Jeff Openden of Northridge, California.

WILL SUPER GLUE STICK TO TEFLON?

e were wary of contacting Loctite and Teflon about this almost metaphysical Imponderable, for it would be like prying a confession from the immovable object (Teflon) and the unstoppable force (Super Glue) that one of their reputations was seriously exaggerated. But we are worldly wise in such matters. After all, we had already cracked the centuries-old conundrum about "If nothing sticks to Teflon, how do they get Teflon to stick to the pan?" in *Why Do Clocks Run Clockwise?* We were ready for a new challenge.

So first we contacted Du Pont, the chemical giant that markets Teflon, a registered trademark for polytetrafluoroethylene (which, for obvious reasons, we'll call ptfe). As we expected, Kenneth Leavell, research supervisor for Du Pont's Teflon/Silverstone division, took a hard line. He firmly holds the conviction that Super Glue won't stick to Teflon, at least "not very well and certainly not reliably." Here are some of the reasons why not:

1. The combination of fluorine and carbon in ptfe forms one of the strongest bonds in the chemical world and one of the most stable.

2. The fluorine atoms around the carbon-fluorine bond are inert, so they form an "impenetrable shield" around the chain of carbon atoms, keeping other chemicals from entering. As Leavell puts it,

> Adhesives need to chemically or physically bond to the substrate to which they are applied. Ptfe contains no chemical sites for other substances to bond with.

3. As we just learned with glue bottles, adhesives need to wet the substrate directly or creep into porous areas in the substrate. But the low surface energy of ptfe prevents wetting and bonding. Leavell compares it to trying to get oil and water to stick together.

And then he lays down the gauntlet:

> Super Glue is "super" because of its speed of cure and relatively strong bonds. As an adhesive for ptfe, it's no better than epoxies, polyurethanes, etc., would be.

So, the immovable object claims near invincibility. How would the unstoppable force react? We contacted Loctite's Richard Palin, technical service adviser. And he folded like a newly cleaned shirt. Yes, Palin admitted, Teflon lacks the cracks necessary for Super Glue to enter in order to bond properly; there would be nowhere for the glue to get into the pan. Yes, he confessed, the critical surface tension is too low for the adhesive to wet the surface. Yes, he broke down in sobs, Super Glue would probably just bead up if applied to a Teflon pan.

Just kidding, actually. Palin -didn't seem upset at all about Super Glue's inability to stick to Teflon. By all accounts, there doesn't seem to be much demand for the task.

Submitted by Bill O'Donnell of Eminence, Missouri.

We trust thermometers. If our temperature is 98.8°, we say we have a fever. But when we take out the thermometer, the temperature reading seems to have no correlation to reality. Why isn't the thermometer sensitive enough to know that room temperature is much lower than 96°, or whatever the lowest number on the thermometer is?

In order to understand this phenomenon, we need a crash course in thermometer anatomy. The metal part of the thermometer that we stick into our mouths is the bulb. The rest of the thermometer is known as the stem. The mercury flows within a capillary, a narrow piece of glass called the mercury column. This column is quite narrow; the mercury in the thermometer is about the width of a human hair. At the base of the mercury column, near the bulb (and the lowest temperature numerals), you'll see a bump, which is called the constriction.

The constriction is the key to how a clinical thermometer works. To create the constriction, one spot of glass is heated to create a bump—controlled warping. The constriction works as a physical impediment to keep mercury from going down toward the bulb unless you shake it. If you don't shake the thermometer, the mercury will only go up, not down. The only reason any temperature in a thermometer rises is that the mercury in the bore of the thermometer expands. When the mercury retracts, the constriction is large enough to stop the flow of mercury.

If you take out your household thermometer and examine its packaging, you will probably see a note that indicates that the thermometer "conforms to ASTM E667." This gibberish refers to the fact that all U.S. manufacturers of thermometers have voluntarily agreed to meet the standards of the American Society for Testing and Materials, an organization that sets standards for many products and services. ASTM is a nonprofit educational association, founded in 1898, that publishes over 7000 separate documents detailing standards in fields ranging from steel and chemicals to robotics, medical devices, and child-resistant packaging. Committees, comprised of volunteers, contribute their time to set standards, and ASTM bylaws require that a majority of committee members may *not* be comprised of producers of the item for which the standards are being set.

The ASTM specifies that clinical thermometers have constrictions, and there is no reason for the industry to want to change the technology; after all, the constriction is cheap and efficient and requires no moving or mechanical parts that could fail to keep the mercury from returning to the bulb. The ASTM standards also help explain why all thermometer scales look so much alike. All clinical thermometers are expected to have scales ranging from at least 96 to 106° Fahrenheit, and graduated in 0.2-degree Fahrenheit intervals. The only long lines allowed on the temperature scale are full-degree gradations and, at the producer's option, the 98.6° designation.

The ASTM also sets minimum standards for the accuracy of clinical thermometers, in degrees Fahrenheit:

Temperature Range	Maximum Error
>96.4	0.4
96.4 to 97.9	0.3

Temperature Range	Maximum Error
98.0 to 101.9	0.2
102.0 to 106	0.3
<106	0.4

A clinical thermometer is designed to retain the body temperature of the user until it is reset, but a thermometer will respond to hotter temperatures. Many a thermometer has been broken in the mistaken belief that it is best to rinse off the bulb by using extremely hot water.

HOW DO THEY MEASURE THE VITAMIN CONTENT OF FOODS?

S ome vitamins are present in such small concentrations in food that there are only a few micrograms (millionths of a gram) of the vitamin per hundred grams of food, while other vitamins might constitute ten milligrams per hundred grams of food. The techniques that work to measure the abundant vitamin often won't work to evaluate the presence of the other.

Jacob Exler, nutritionist for the Nutrient Data Research Branch of the Human Nutrition Information Service, told *Imponderables* that there are two types of analytical procedures to measure the vitamin content of foods, chemical and microbiological:

> The chemical procedures measure the actual amount of a vitamin or a derivative of the vitamin, and the microbiological procedures measure the biological activity of the vitamin on some selected organism.

Today, chemical procedures are in vogue. In the past,

microbiological studies were more common, and researchers tested not only on bacteria but on live rats. In fact, as late as the 1970s, the FDA used approximately twenty thousand rats a year just to test foods for vitamin D content! Roger E. Coleman, of the National Food Processors Association, explains the theory behind microbiological studies:

> An older but still very acceptable method for vitamin assay is to measure the amount of microbiological growth a food supports. There are certain bacteria that require an outside source of one or more vitamins to grow. The growth of these bacteria is proportional to the amount of the required vitamin in the food.

But microbiological work is extremely sensitive. If conditions are not perfect, results can be skewed. As an example, an article in *FDA Papers* states that "the organism used for measuring vitamin B12 activity will show a measurable response when dosed with less than one ten-billionth of a gram of the vitamin." Microbiological assays work more effectively than chemical methods for measuring B12 levels (and some other vitamins, such as biotin, B6) because chemical analysis isn't sensitive enough to respond to the minute amounts of the vitamin contained in food.

In a chemical analysis, each vitamin in a given food must be measured separately. There are many chemical procedures to choose from, with catchy names like "gas-liquid chromatography" and "infrared spectroscopy." Coleman explains a few different types of chemical analysis that are a little more comprehensible:

> Each measuring technique is based on a property of the vitamin. For example, riboflavin fluoresces [produces light when exposed to radiant energy] and is measured by a fluorometer or fluorescence detector. Vitamin C combines with a certain purple dye and makes it colorless. By measuring the amount of this dye that is changed from purple to colorless, we can calculate the amount of vitamin C present.

Despite the high-tech names, chemical analysis microbiological methods, but it is cheaper and faster—and doesn't necessitate twenty thousand rats a year sacrificing their life for vitamin D.

Submitted by Violet Wright of Hobbes, New Mexico. Thanks also to Todd Grooten of Kalamazoo, Michigan.

If Richard Feynman and Albert Einstein can't stamp out all the Imponderables of the world, do you expect us to do it? But we're nothing if not persistent. Keep sending in your Imponderables about every conceivable subject—they're the lifeblood of these books.

If you're the first person to send in an Imponderable we use in a book, you'll receive an acknowledgment and a free autographed copy for your contribution.

Although we accept "snail mail," we strongly encourage you to e-mail us if possible. Because of the volume of mail, we can't always provide a personal response to every letter, but we'll try—a self-addressed stamped envelope doesn't hurt. We're much better about answering e-mail, although we fall behind when we're in heavy work mode.

Come visit us online at the Imponderables Web site, where you can pose Imponderables, read our blog, and find out what's happening at

Imponderables Central. Send your correspondence, along with your name, address, and (optional) phone number to:

Feldman@imponderables.com
http://www.imponderables.com
or
Imponderables
P.O. Box 116
Planetarium Station
New York, NY 10024-0116